AF764802

Get Funded

Learn High Probability Day Trading Methods to Pass Prop Firm Challenges and Become a Funded Trader

J.T. WELLESLEY

Published by FB Media LLC, New Mexico.

CONTENTS

CHAPTER 1
THE CHALLENGE

Trading is by far one of the most challenging things you will ever attempt. It can also be one of the most rewarding. For many people, once you've traded, you can never look back. It will change the way you see the world, the behavior patterns of people, and all the ways you will understand chance and success in life.

Trading is unique. It's the epitome of a world where your status is 100% based on merit. Success as a trader is based entirely on your performance and ability.

As a beginner, it will feel like an uphill battle, day in and day out... but when it clicks for you, it's the best feeling in the world. You made money because you performed well.

The markets will teach you so much about yourself, your true self when no one else is around, and human behavior.

The more you learn as a trader, the more you will learn about how the world inherently works, for better or worse. You will be changed by it.

I began my journey in a very different way than many of the traders in the world: I began my career as a dealer at a retail forex broker in the early 2000s.

It was an era of unregulated firms taking advantage of the ignorance of customers, and operating under a dealing desk business model that directly profited from the losses of the customer traders.

Part of my job was to manage the company's exposure. That was the fancy way of describing the very ethically questionable task of making sure that when the company's customers made money, we had to do everything possible to either reduce the chances of the customer's success or quickly neutralize the situation by placing an equivalent trade with the company's liquidity providers (it was sort of like trading in a brokerage account with a larger company, called a prime broker, held by the company... except we only placed trades to protect ourselves in case the customer made money.)

If you're a beginner to the world of financial markets, this might be shocking to you... or maybe it's not surprising in the least, considering the portrayal of Wall Street in both the mainstream and alternative media over the recent decades.

Today, similar broker business models still exist, mainly operating under entities that are domiciled offshore and, in many cases, no longer accepting business from traders in the United States.

When I left my position as a dealer, the regulatory environment in the US had just begun to shift. It was a landslide of changes, with new capital requirements and strict registration requirements, causing the vast majority of the US-based retail forex brokers to effectively close up shop and head overseas for business.

Within a couple of years, we went from hundreds of retail forex brokers across America down to three: OANDA, FXCM, and Gain Capital (aka. Forex.com.)

Interactive Brokers, of course, remained active and were technically a legitimate alternative but their business model never fully relied on the retail forex business and, at the time, catered to traders with larger minimum capital.

From the perspective of the first generation of retail forex brokers - the people you could appropriately consider the villains of the story - it was the end of a golden era.

For me, on the other hand, it was a journey into a new path within the industry: I voluntarily jumped into the point-of-view of the people I spent years trading against. I became a trader.

Bringing my undying fascination with the world of trading in financial markets, I ventured into my next chapter as a fund manager.

The company I worked for was a proprietary trading firm (or "prop firm" for short) but when I say that today, beginners have a very different idea of the type of work I did and my position in the company.

These days, the term "prop firm" is likely to refer to a type of company that offers evaluation accounts (with demo accounts, aka. paper trading or "virtual" accounts) for a fee. If you pass an evaluation, you are given the chance to trade using the company's capital (which may still be virtual.) These trader evaluation prop firms are the types of companies that this book is about... but they're not the type I traded for back then.

The reasons I chose this path with a prop firm of old, however, were similar. As an individual trader, I had limited capital to trade.

There was a big difference between managing the risk of customer positions at a broker and trading with my own money. The psychological difference was the obvious part. Arguably worse was were the trading conditions, such as the lack of ability to "make the spread" (profit from the difference between the bid and ask rather than paying it.) That was the case in forex, at least. On futures, which are traded on exchanges, it was a different situation but still far more difficult than directly playing against retail traders.

This was, of course, long before micro futures contracts came into existence. So, it was a choice between trading way too large for my own capital with the futures contracts available at the time, or trading with an inherent disadvantage in the retail forex market.

At the time, there were two types of prop firms in

existence. The upper tier were the real competitors in the market - firms who hire based on extremely tough criteria that the vast majority of retail customers on the message boards back then (YouTube and social media today) would never qualify to work for. Beneath them were education vendors who also acted as veiled broker-dealers. Those were far less strict in their criteria because they usually worked to attract retail traders with their education material and demanded risk capital deposits which were just disguised forms of margin deposits. This is not to deride those companies, however. Many were of great value to customers who lacked capital, and they offered a lot of benefits such as lower commission fees, at the time (back when commissions at retail brokers across the US were extremely expensive.)

The company I worked for was a bit of a hybrid. There was a clear divide in the company between the real traders, who were there to manage the company's capital, and the retail traders, who were essentially broker-dealer customers with privileges. I was hired to manage firm capital. In reality, my job was to control risk for the firm's accounts based on my experience at the retail forex dealing desk.

Working at a prop firm meant trading with "OPM" (other people's money) again. It also meant I could play a surrogate market maker role again at times.

It was a different experience from my days at a forex broker despite the similarities in my duties.

Over the years, I met many successful traders who

went from individual retail traders - with no institutional or professional background - to full-time pros based on their acquired ability. And, of course, there were many traders who struggled to stay just above break-even while the company continued to collect markups on fees and commissions from their trading activity.

In both cases, I came to respect the traders on a different level than many of my peers.

Being a trader is a unique position to be in. It's never been about asking their boss for a raise or a bonus. It's all about perseverance, dedication, and performance.

At this firm, some traders were "remote" - meaning they would trade from home. Others traded at the company's in-person trading floor. Their positions were the same - independent contractors who are actually customers of the company - but their work environment and experiences with the company were drastically different.

I spoke to so many remote traders who became frustrated with what felt to them like running in circles chasing an unachievable goal, even after a brief period of profitability. They became jaded and pessimistic that any strategy in the world could ever work consistently for anyone. Some of them quit. Others took some more time... and then quit. Many of them were retail traders who became remote prop traders who never stepped foot on an in-person trading floor at any point in their lives.

On the flip side, I also met many traders who were

in exactly the same place early on, but they persevered... and eventually, some of them found what worked for them. A large percentage of those had chosen to trade in-person at the firm's trading floor, either from the beginning or for part of their journey.

The difference between the remote and trading floor traders was the ability to see, by working next to peers, that it can be done.

This isn't to say that trading in person at a classic prop firm was a magic solution. It's simply my observation that with enough exposure to other people on the same trading floor - some of whom were consistently profitable - comes a different perspective.

Around the same time, I often saw the same pattern of behavior on the internet forums as with remote prop traders at the time. Traders who had put in the work for years would become jaded and reply to beginners that there was no hope. It was all a mirage. The brokers, the banks, the prop firms, Wall Street itself - they're all out to get you. It's all rigged.

On that front, they're not entirely wrong. It's just a little too black-and-white of a perspective. It's akin to a college athlete spending years honing their ability, then failing to make it to a professional league, and coming to the conclusion that the entire sport is rigged against him or her. Well, the challenges are definitely there and the people who succeed are certainly exploiting all of the possible opportunities to outperform these people, but it's not a brick wall. And, thankfully for traders, there's far less of a performance reduction from age.

The truth is that institutions and other "smart money" participants are not as god-like as retail traders make them out to be.

The "smart money" players face losses too. For every successful hedge fund that retail traders like to demonize for rigging the game against them, there are hundreds that failed and disappeared without you having heard of them - like businesses of all kinds.

The same goes for brokers, banks, prop firms, and every other type of business on Wall Street. They're not invincible. They're just playing the game to the best of their ability, and usually, with the capital that they raise, they're able to play with a head start.

Having traded on both sides of the proverbial fence in this industry, I came to understand the reality of the markets early on.

I've witnessed traders employing strategies that benefited from opportunities I understood to exist, yet those traders had no idea why their strategy had an edge. They just figured out how to trade it. They knew that it worked but they had no clue about why.

It's made me more open to the possibility that a person who trades a strategy - bearing no resemblance to anything I would trade - may be exploiting the same opportunity in the markets. The only difference is, if and when those strategies lose their edge in the markets, those who trade based on untrue assumptions might have a much harder time finding a new edge.

This is why I encourage beginners and advanced

traders alike to learn how their trading strategies work and why.

If you're just starting out now, as a beginner trader, or you're struggling to become a consistently profitable one, just know that it can be done.

It will be a rewarding journey... but it will not be easy.

People love to say that 95% of traders lose money. Well, based on the percentages released by some brokers, it seems the real percentages are closer to somewhere between 70% and 85%, depending on which broker. As it turns out, 70% to 90% of small businesses fail within five years. And, according to the US Bureau of Labor Statistics, at least 70% of all businesses fail eventually.

Likewise, the majority of athletes will never play professionally. 93% of SAG-AFTRA (the union for actors in Hollywood) are not making a living wage from acting.

As an individual, none of those stats should deter you. If you feel that you truly have potential to be one of the successful minority, the only way you can guarantee failure is by giving up. As long as you have other sources of income before you become consistently profitable, there's no real reason to throw in the towel. You won't be too old or injured to run on this field or be cast in this role.

The beauty of trading is that you, as an individual, have the same opportunity to succeed (and to fail) as any given hedge fund, bank, or other big business... you might just be doing it at a fraction of the size in terms of dollar figures. But in percentage terms, you have an opportunity to make a good living from it if it's what you want from it.

The problem is that most people are introduced to this business by the idea of trading as easy money. It's like walking onto a court in the NBA and thinking, "Oh, it's easy to throw a ball into a net," and then being disappointed that you couldn't become the next Michael Jordan because you learned to play the game for less than a year, only know how to play offense with no concept of defense, and still get confused every time an opponent telegraphs doing one thing but really intended to do the opposite.

If easy money is your expectation from the markets, then maybe this field really isn't for you.

If you have the drive to learn, to improve, and to become the best you can be within this crazy game of humans exchanging money for assets, maybe trading is for you.

It's hard. It's unforgiving. But it won't take you down because you were born with the wrong last name or happen to lack business contacts in a particular industry. It will take you down because, like life itself, it won't take anything easy on you.

It's up to you to get back up and keep trying.

It will force you to confront your own personality in ways you had never considered before. There will be struggles against your confidence in your strategy, your confidence in yourself, and your beliefs in many things you assume to be true.

That is the challenge. And if you are still excited to take it head-on, you are already ahead of your peers.

CHAPTER 2
PROP FIRMS

In 2023, one of the largest retail forex brokers in Europe, IG Markets UK, had a total of 117,400 customer accounts. In the same year, one of the largest prop firms in Europe, FTMO, had 960,000 accounts. It's no wonder why OANDA, one of the most successful (and last remaining) retail brokers in the US, recently launched their prop firm too.

Today's prop firms are a natural and logical offspring of the broker-dealer education vendor generation that I worked with in the past.

These new prop firms allow retail traders to subscribe to evaluation accounts of a particular size, usually anywhere from $10,000 to $250,000 in notional balances. By trading in demo (or paper trading) accounts, traders must abide by specific rules in order to pass an evaluation, hoping to graduate to an account where a percentage of profits (often shared with the firm) can be withdrawn.

It's a variation of a tried and tested business model used by a much older entity, one that controls more capital than any single bank or hedge fund: the government of the United States of America.

The country offers newcomers a chance at the potential of success and freedom from the restrictions of others, in exchange for payment (initially, immigration filing fees.) Those who succeed will split their earnings (in the form of state and federal taxes, which sometimes also include a subscription fee component) in exchange for the privilege of leveraging the nation's resources.

In both cases, there are rules you're expected to abide by. Those rules are arguably well-meaning but they can pose unique challenges to individuals.

Like the prop firms of the past, the appeal is the opportunity to trade with a larger capital base. This is not insignificant. As many intermediate-level traders have likely noticed, the skills learned as a beginner - if you survive the early period of losses - come with the experience and knowledge to understand that risk management is a vital part of the game.

And, in major institutions, it's common for per-trade risk is usually around 0.2% of capital or less.

For a retail trader, having to trade such tiny percentages of their own capital would mean - at best - making enough money to buy coffee, even if you were a world-class, naturally talented level of trader.

By trading with the sizes of accounts offered by prop firms, you gain access to a way to trade nominal sizes that most beginners simply could not trade without a high likelihood of losing an entire account to a small streak of inevitable losing trades.

So, what's the catch?

The early offerings from this generation of prop firms had much stricter, more restrictive rules. These rules, ostensibly designed to control risk, were often nearly impossible to overcome - even for very skilled traders. In general, you would find very tight loss limits, wide profit targets, short time limits to pass evaluations, strict limits on types of trading strategies, and more.

Thankfully, as the industry evolved, many of these rules have been relaxed.

As of this writing, it's less common for today's prop firms to have a time limit on evaluations. This rule change alone is a major improvement for traders who have mastered risk management skills. It allows you to build toward the profit target without trading like a gambler.

Depending on where you live, the types of prop firms may also be limited. In the US, futures prop firms are your only option at present. In Europe, you may also be able to trade forex and CFDs. (Based on my background in the world of forex and CFDs, I wouldn't necessarily classify that as an advantage... but if you know you are capable of navigating those turbulent waters, those firms can be a valid opportunity for you.)

Choosing a prop firm is not just about comparing the price and size of their evaluation accounts.

Take some time to research and learn about all of the rules currently in place. Be sure that the firm's rules fit your trading style, ability, and talents.

If you happen to specialize in scalping and you see that a prop firm clearly states "no scalping" then that's an obvious no. If you usually trade on a higher timeframe and hold most positions for at least a few minutes or longer, then that's not a problem for you. As a scalper, there are plenty of other firms who do allow scalping, so they would be a better choice.

On the flip side, the majority of futures prop firms do not allow overnight positions. (This is a practical choice on the side of the prop firms, especially in futures in the US, where initial margin requirements are much higher than day trading margin minimums.) If you're a day trader, such rules are of no concern to you. If you're a swing trader, on the other hand, that would be a problem.

After you've done your due diligence on the prop firm's rules and feel that they're likely to be a good fit for you and your style of trading, the main objective of every evaluation account is to hit the profit target while avoiding the loss limit.

For most beginners, this can be challenging. If you're still a beginner who hasn't achieved consistent profitability, be honest with yourself and practice using a demo account on your own first.

Being able to trade a demo account profitability doesn't guarantee you can do so in a live account or a prop firm evaluation account. But if you can't trade profitably even on a demo, then you definitely won't have the ability to trade live or in a prop firm evaluation.

So, take the first step and prove to yourself that you can trade successfully in a demo account first.

In theory, evaluation accounts' profit targets and loss limits are a fair way to assess traders because risk management is an important part of trading professionally. Any long-term profitable strategy should be able to stick within loss limits most of the time, even if it may be challenging.

However, be aware that the standard - as of the time of this writing - is for the loss limit to trail your profits. This is similar to the concept of a trailing stop loss, which moves up at certain increments as your trade moves into unrealized profits, the trailing loss limit will move as you make gains in your prop firm evaluation account.

For example, if your evaluation is a $50,000 account with a loss limit of $3000, then your minimum balance would be $47,000. (This means that if your balance drops below $47,000, you fail the evaluation.) If it's a trailing loss limit, which it usually is, that means that if you go $100 into profit (ie. you reach $50,100 in equity), your new minimum is $47,100.

Depending on your style of trading, this may make

it extremely challenging to pass an evaluation, or it may not be much of an issue for you.

Most traders find it necessary to trade smaller sizes in order to dodge the trailing loss limit. If you're extremely patient and know you can do it consistently, this can work for you. But for most, this can be a far too conservative approach, so I'll get into better ways to optimize your trade sizes in this book.

Additionally, typical prop firm evaluation accounts have asymmetrical profit targets and loss limits. For example: a $6000 profit target and a $3000 loss limit. This means that, with all else being equal, you are twice as likely to hit the loss limit as you are to reach the profit target. It means that in order to pass this type of account, your Expected Value (EV) must be very high. Most traders simply do not have the ability to achieve that high of an EV.

Meanwhile, some prop firms offer account types (usually with smaller balances) with symmetrical loss limits and profit targets. For example, a $1500 profit target and a $1500 loss limit are offered on some $25,000 accounts. While $25,000 is on the smaller end of prop firm accounts, it may be worth considering starting with these accounts if you can't realistically hit a 2-to-1 or higher difference between the evaluation profit target and loss limit.

If you hit a loss limit and fail an evaluation, it's not the end of the road. You can either pay for an evaluation reset before the next renewal - which is usually a lower fee than the regular price of evaluations

- or wait for the next monthly renewal, which usually means automatically resetting failed evaluations.

Ideally, you should always aim to avoid hitting the loss limits. It will cost you less if you avoid it and also reinforce better trading habits. But I also understand that there are time, monetary, and opportunity cost considerations that make this sort of approach impractical.

This is why it's worth being aware of the time of month that you initially signed up for your evaluation account, so you know how far away the potential reset is from the current date. (For example, if you happen to be in the middle of a large drawdown, 3 days from the next renewal, which allows a reset without an additional reset fee, it's a different situation from the same drawdown 20 days away from the next renewal.) I'll go into some strategies to approach these situations in this book.

Also, be sure to take into consideration what the prop firm's profit split percentage is.

It's not always a bad thing for prop firms to take a percentage of your profits after you pass the evaluation - it helps to place the firm on your side that way because they will make some money when you make money.

There are situations where some firms still place you on demo accounts and don't copy your trades to the real market even after you pass an evaluation - those are equivalent to "B-Book" retail forex brokers who benefit from your losses. If you are trading with a firm that either gives you direct access to a live account or operates with an STP (Straight Through Processing, in retail forex terms) type of business model, then your gains would not be the firm's losses. In such a situation, profit shares only add to the ways that the firm's interests are shared with your own. You are less likely to be rejected in withdrawal requests at such firms.

A few older prop firms still require a multi-step qualification process where you would have to pass more than one phase before qualifying for an account that allows you to withdraw profits. This is becoming increasingly rare among today's prop firms, but it was fairly common a few years ago and may still be the case in some companies. Look into whether your prop firm of choice is one of them so you know what you're facing during the qualification phase.

Carefully read all of the rules and be aware of what you can and can't do. It wouldn't be pleasant to find out after believing you passed an evaluation that you had violated clear rules in the process. If you're a beginner, learn the meanings of some of the restrictions and requirements if you are not familiar with them. If you have any doubt about what a rule means, ask the prop firm's support staff before you go ahead and buy evaluation accounts.

Last but not least, consider purchasing multiple smaller accounts rather than one large one.

For example, if you were planning to purchase one $200,000 account, consider buying two $100,000 accounts instead. Or if you were planning to buy a

$100,000 account originally, then consider buying two $50,000 accounts instead.

It may cost you approximately the same or less to purchase multiple smaller accounts. The benefit is that you would be giving yourself more chances to pass the evaluation in any given time period. It's one additional way to increase your probability of success.

As a word of warning: It may be tempting to place opposite trades in two accounts as a way to win in one and lose in the other. There are multiple reasons that this is a bad idea. Firstly, the prop firm can easily tell what you are attempting to do (especially if they are two accounts at the same firm) and it is likely against the rules. This is a fair rule because no firm, even if they are 100% legitimately seeking good traders, would want traders who just game the system by taking two opposite trades in separate accounts. That doesn't make you a good trader and anyone can do it. Secondly, if you attempt this, you still need some level of skill to be able to do it consistently because it won't benefit you if you lose one trade in account A while winning one in account B, then win one in account A while losing in account B. That just puts you back at square one. You would need a consistent way to have the two accounts go in opposite directions. And, if you attempt this using a one-trade approach, you would likely violate the consistency rule at most firms, which, again, is a fair rule for similar reasons in this context.

Prop firms are not a way to game the system or a way for beginner traders to fake their way into trading larger accounts, because chances are, if you thought of it, so did the owners of the prop firm.

Instead, focus on becoming a good trader first, then use this opportunity to make your trades count for your bottom line in a way that they simply can't if you trade with your own capital. Do your research on each company before you attempt to pass their evaluation, and choose account types that suit your abilities. After that, prop firms can be an amazing opportunity to take your trading to the next level.

CHAPTER 3
EXPECTED VALUE (EV)

Entire businesses thrive by operating with positive Expected Value (EV) and taking money from people who don't. Lotteries, casino games, many types of insurance, and warranties on affordably replaceable products have one thing in common: they all make money because humans do not intuitively judge probability correctly. It's nothing to be ashamed of if you have been one of those people because it's a natural part of human instincts that make these businesses viable.

Trading is a game of chance.

When I say this, traders often become defensive about the idea that their chosen profession is being compared to gambling. Well, life is also a game of chance. Some people begin with hundreds of millions and others are dealt nothing at first. Luckily, we don't live in a time where the only way to achieve wealth is through inheritance or a family's social standing. Often, those who have struggled financially are the same people who are the best at taking charge of their lives and creating success out of the resources they do have. This is what trading is at its best.

Yet, as in life, for every good that you seek within the game, you should also consider the risks. Sometimes, these are opportunity risks. Other times, these are real monetary risks or the risk of wasting time that you will never recover.

The worst thing that can happen to a beginner trader is a lucky streak before learning the foundations of the markets and expected value.

That lucky crypto trade that made millions; that lucky stock trade that happened to be the bottom before a massive move upward. It tends to cause a type of confidence in the illusion of ability when anyone could have done it at the right time and place. It's great that these things can happen... but they didn't happen in a way that helps you become a good trader. Instead, it tends to make people over-confident in their low level of experience and ability. If you experience something like this and you never trade again, that's great. It's the same thing a lottery winner or roulette winner should do.

If you then decide to trade full-time, however... know that there's a long road ahead of you.

Many people who got lucky that way will lose all of

it back because they never even learned the basics before getting lucky.

THE TRUE VALUE OF EV

So, what exactly is Expected Value and what does it mean to have an edge?

When traders first learn of the concept of EV or expectancy, there's a tendency to associate it with mechanical trading strategies or automation. Certainly, a positive EV can be found in those approaches but there are also plenty of mechanical and automated strategies with a negative EV.

For manual traders, your EV is your real measurement of success.

As with a baseball player's batting average, the EV of a manual trader is not static. In reality, mechanical strategies also do not have a static EV either, because market conditions change. In both cases, that's okay. The only necessity is that you adapt and maintain a positive EV.

A positive EV is a measurable edge in the game of trading. It's the difference between the casino (positive EV) and the gambler (negative EV.)

To measure if you have an edge during any given time period, use the following formula:

EV = (Average Win Size x Win Rate) - (Average Loss Size x Loss Rate)

Average Loss Size: The average amount in dollars that you lose in your average losing trade.

Average Win Size: The average amount in dollars that you win in your average winning trade.

Win Rate: The percentage of your trades that you win.

Loss Rate: 1 - Win Rate (One minus your win rate). You don't have to track loss rate separately, you can calculate it from your win rate. So, if your win rate is 0.66 (66%), then your loss rate is:

1 - 0.66 = 0.34

This is because your win rate is the percentage of your trades won, so the loss rate is literally the opposite slice out of the 100% of trades you took.

The result is the average expected amount (positive or negative) you should expect from each trade or bet.

If your EV is 1.00, then it means that if you trade many times repeatedly with your strategy - assuming market conditions remain similar to the conditions during your sample of data - you should expect to win $1.00 per trade.

If your EV is a negative number, you should expect to lose money over the long run. Even if you control your risk very well, it would, at best, slow down the process of losing money.

Why does EV matter?

When was the last time you heard of someone playing roulette professionally? Now consider how many casinos that operate roulette wheels are still standing, making millions of dollars per year.

Yet the casino only holds a small edge (a very small positive EV) in the game of roulette... the law of large numbers ensures that they'll always come out on top. This is why a player with a positive EV should lean toward more repetition while a player with negative or questionable EV should cut back.

You might have been taught that you shouldn't over-trade. This is partly because some strategies only work under certain circumstances and times of day, in which case, it's a valid piece of advice for a trader with a positive EV. However, more often, it is because vendors are selling mechanical strategies that have negative EV and they are relying on you to trade less so that your lucky trades can reinforce the illusion.

For the casinos and lottery commissions, it's the opposite. Repetition is beneficial. Every customer who plays their games is drawn in by the theoretical "possibility" of an outsized payoff.

In the short term, even a player without a real edge could still win, sometimes even win big, on the odd occasion. This works in favor of the parties on the opposite side - the house, which has a small edge - since it tends to trigger added confidence in the uneducated players, leading them to continue wasting their money on a dream that goes against the laws of nature.

The majority of lottery players are precisely the most uneducated and undercapitalized. They are the people who could least afford to play in the first place. And the few who get lucky enough to win big tend to be the types of people who lose all of it very quickly (mostly due to a lack of quality financial education in the school system.) The optimal play for a lucky lottery winner is to never play again.

The game of American roulette offers a player a 1 in 38 chance of winning 35 times the amount wagered. (As a result, there's a 37 in 38 chance of losing the amount wagered.)

Now, Joe walks into a casino and wants to place a $1 bet - after all, that 35-to-1 reward-to-risk factor looks like the chance to win $35 with it is well worth the risk, right? Let's plug his information into the EV formula to see how it works out:

$$EV = (-\$1 \times (37/38)) + (\$35 \times (1/38))$$
$$EV = -0.9737 + 0.9210$$
$$EV = -0.0526$$

Joe's expected value in the bet is -0.0526, which can be rounded to a loss of -$0.05 per wager he places. What this translates to is that, over time, if Joe were to repeatedly place the same wager 100 times, he'll lose approximately $5.26.

The casino has a house edge of 5.26%.

Of course, in the short term, it's entirely possible that Joe could get lucky and actually win. He might even get lucky enough to come out on top... which is why every casino is designed with two major goals in mind: Firstly, they'll do everything in their power to lure their customers to stay as long as possible because they understand that the law of large numbers is what will cause that -5.26% EV to take its effect. Secondly, they want as many different customers as possible - after all, poor Joe can only lose so much of his money before he's done. Other customers with the same lack of regard for nature's basic math rules must follow in his footsteps... and Vegas exists because that's exactly what happens day in and day out.

Sportsbooks run a similar business. They allow their customers to bet on the outcomes of sporting events. Like financial markets, the perceived probability of a sporting event's outcome will change according to newly available information.

While a stigma surrounds all forms of "gambling," the reality is that betting on sports is a closely related business in many ways to trading in financial markets. In fact, I've worked with people in the retail forex business who came from the offshore sports betting industry. (After all, they were already in the business of profiting from the law of large numbers.)

For instance, in basketball, bettors must wager based on a handicap. If Team A were an underdog against Team B, the sports books may open the line at Team B -5 (which is Team A +5), meaning bets on Team A would win as long as Team A loses by less than 5 points (bets on Team B would win if Team B wins by more than 5 points.) Only if the game ends with Team B winning by exactly 5 points, in this example, would the wagers simply be returned to bettors - called a "push."

A hypothetically "fair" payoff for a handicap with a 50/50 probability would pay $100 for every $100 wagered. However, the sports book has to pocket a little profit, so the actual payoff would be more like $91 for every $100 wagered. In order words, no matter which outcome may happen (with the exception of a push, in which everyone will be back to where they began before wagers were placed) the sports book will pocket 9% of every wager on either side.

In reality, the true probability of Team B defeating Team A by exactly 5 points may not be 50%. However, that handicap line is the aggregate result of the Vegas sports books receiving wagers on both sides and they will often move the line if "too much action" comes in on one side. Sound familiar? They're market makers, and their job is to simply take the "vigorish" (the "spread" in financial markets terms) as their profit.

While there are better-informed individuals and organizations (syndicates, essentially the sports betting equivalent of "smart money" in the markets) who often manage to assess the probabilities better than the Vegas sports books themselves, the majority of "casual" customers will simply bet on their favorite team regardless of the handicap's probabilities (the equivalent of beginners who attempt to trade every time a moving average crosses over.)

Returning to Joe in our example, after losing a few hundred on the roulette wheel, convinced that his luck "has got to turn around after that," walks over to the sports book at the same casino with his last $50 in his pocket. He sees that the line for a Lakers game is being offered and he's always been a fan of the Lakers. In fact, the line quoted is Lakers -4. He, of course, has never done a statistical analysis in his entire life, let alone able to really assess the probability of the Lakers winning by more than 4 points against their particular opponents in this game. All he knows is that he thinks the Lakers will win and he thinks they're good enough to win by 4 points or more, so he puts his last $50 on the Lakers -4 line.

If he gets lucky, chances are he'll be compelled to do it again sometime in the future with just as much in-depth statistical research. In fact, even if he doesn't, hundreds of others like him will do the same - keeping the sports book in business.

The importance of this example is that no one can know with 100% certainty that the handicap on any particular sporting event has exactly 50/50 probability. Enough "action" (bets) from the syndicates (smart money) might indicate the accuracy of the line better than the opening line (opening price) offered by the same sportsbook the previous day.

And that's the point: The sportsbooks don't know for 100% certainty that their handicap line is the correct 50/50 probability point from the moment they open their books. However, their "vigorish," which may range from 10% down to as little as 5%, is more than enough of an edge to ensure long-term profitability.

As in financial markets, the dealers and market makers do not always know the exact probabilities. Both the financial markets and sports aren't roulette wheels. Instead, the goal on the side of the dealers or sportsbooks is to profit from the spread (the vig for sportsbooks.)

Most beginner traders are the equivalent of "casual" players at the sportsbooks.

Worse yet, most retail traders gravitate toward using that high leverage to scalp on the microscopic timeframes. For instance, they may risk 5 pips in hopes of making 5 pips.

At first, it may seem like their strategy has a 50% probability of winning - and that's optimistic even if there were no spread. However, granting them the hypothetical possibility that their average trade has a probability of 50%, even the lowest spread possible would give them a very negative EV to overcome.

So, for every 5-pip trade such a trader makes, at least 0.5 pips are lost in the spread. (Retail brokers never truly allow buying at the bid or selling at the offer - they only fill your orders when the market trades through your order.) By nature, that's a 10% edge loss so every trade would require an edge greater than 60/40 to break even. And, in reality, most over-leveraged traders doing this don't even understand the concept of testing for probability, let alone be able to consistently execute trades with such a significant edge.

The law of large numbers, of course, will inevitably

drain their account - and they'll likely have been convinced by others that if only they mastered their psychology, they could win it all back and more. Psychology can destroy any strategy, even one with an edge... but no amount of psychology can turn a negative expectancy into a positive one.

It's no wonder retail forex brokers were all so tempted to capitalize on this reality by simply taking the opposite sides of their own customers' trades. Even without manipulation or any other issue related to the conflict of interest, their spread combined with the customers' lack of understanding about the law of large numbers (and how it relates to the spread in no-edge trades) is more than enough to ensure their bonuses.

Does this mean you should never trade the low time frames? No. It just means it's harder to maintain a positive expectancy in those time frames. If you are able to develop a scalping style that manages to do it, then you should definitely trade it.

Just be aware that it's a steeper mountain you are climbing if you're not already locked into a scalping strategy.

THE RISK-REWARD/WIN RATE DYNAMIC

It's possible for bad risk management to destroy a good strategy, but it's impossible for good risk management to turn a losing strategy into a profitable one.

However, it's also worth taking into account that,

depending on the nature of your strategy, a good risk management method may be able to help your EV **as long as you are still able to retain the same win rate**.

"Always trade with good risk-reward" sounds good to beginners, and vendors love to use it, but it's not as easy as it sounds.

With all else being equal, in trading all financial markets:

- a better risk-reward (lower risk, higher profit) reduces your win rate
- a worse risk-reward (higher risk, lower profit) increases your win rate

Again, this is just the default dynamic between risk-reward and win rate, the critical ingredients of EV.

This means that if you flip a coin to decide whether to go long or short, at random times of day and using random instruments, your win rate would go up if you risk bigger stop losses for smaller profit targets and it would go down if you risk smaller stop losses for bigger targets.

Your job as a professional trader is to operate as the casino, not the gambler: Trade when you have a real edge - a positive EV. While you have a positive EV, repetition is the key. Let the law of large numbers work it out for you.

The challenge is knowing where and when your positive EV exists. For many strategies, your positive EV is specific to a certain time of day or certain market conditions. It's rarely universal unless you are combining multiple types of trading.

If you start with a positive EV but then continue trading and find that it turns negative, take time away from the markets to reassess your strategy. Was there a particular circumstance that made your winning trades win and losing trades lose? Were your losing trades simply a short-term run of losses that should be considered inevitable for your style of trading? These are all specific issues with your own approach to trading that should be explored each time it appears you've lost your edge.

So, how do you track your EV?

TRACKING YOUR EV

To start, trade half of the size you would based on your risk management method.

Don't confuse this first stage with actual trading. Preferably, you should do this with a demo account first, but I know many of you would prefer to do it with a live account or a prop firm evaluation account. Psychologically, it's difficult to treat a demo account with no stakes the same way as you would treat an account with real money or real potential to pass a prop firm evaluation.

Either way, at this stage, the purpose is to gather real-world statistics of what happens when you combine:

- your strategy; with

- you as a trader; and
- the current market conditions

Those three elements have never met in one place before. Your first task is to get them acquainted and see what happens first.

Each week, calculate your EV.

This means tracking the average size of your winning trades, the average size of losing trades, and your win rate. (Recall that your loss rate can be calculated with 1 minus win rate. So, if you are winning 55% of trades, then win rate is 0.55 and loss rate is 1 - 0.55 = 0.45.)

It's okay if it's negative at first. It's better to know this ahead of time than to trade blindly, hoping that you will be profitable when you won't.

Your goal is to at least be able to bring your initial EV to a small positive number.

Do this for at least 2 weeks. (If you have the discipline, then do it for a full month, but I know most beginners won't be able to do it for that long yet.)

For many beginners, streaks of good luck or bad luck can heavily distort your perception of this initial stage if it's too short. Don't let that happen. Instead, trade small enough to not lose too much money (or to not waste a prop firm evaluation you paid for) and use the experience to gather the data you need to determine your starting point.

As you trade each day, continue to plug those numbers into the EV formula.

If you still have a positive EV at the end of each week, continue trading. If not, re-assess what may have changed.

If you trade two or more entirely different strategies, continue to reassess the EV of each strategy separately.

If one strategy's EV goes positive, you can employ a normal sizing method such as one of the systematic risk management concepts. If it drops negative, reduce exposure to that strategy or consider pausing it until you have a reason to believe the assumptions of the strategy's design may be applicable to current market conditions again.

Keep tracking your EV this way to know which strategies are still working for you and which ones are not.

Most importantly, don't just take the EV formula as a given. Look at its components. If it's not already intuitive to you, try to really look at why it works the way it does.

It's taking "how likely you are to make your average win" and subtracting "the likelihood that you'll lose your average loss size."

If you understand this, then you'll understand why it's important to keep track of your own EV for each strategy you employ.

It's important to know and understand your risks and opportunities in the market. Some market conditions make particular types of trading strategies difficult to maintain profitability. Other market conditions make it seem too easy.'

Also, get to know what types of strategies work for you as a trader.

Whether you trade manually, automated, or semi-automated, this still holds true. Your ability to stomach the size, type, and distribution of losing trades (how often they happen and how they're spread out) - because losses are inevitable - will determine whether that strategy will work for you.

Your goal is to become a successful independent contractor to a prop firm that offers the type of accounts suitable for your approach. So, trade your trading plan the way you would execute a business plan. Be the house, not the player.

CHAPTER 4
RISK TO WIN

Most beginners have already been preached to - by everyone from trading educators and YouTubers to fellow traders on social media - about the critical importance of risk management. If you're new to trading and you haven't already heard the religious dogma about what you must "always" or "never" do in risk management for trading, you probably will soon. Thankfully, that's not what this chapter is about.

The most successful traders, as with many of the most successful people in life, are those who can accept losses on the way to success - because losses, no matter how big or small, are inevitable. That part is true. And that part will probably be repeated so many times to you in trading communities that you'll want to throw something the next time someone says it.

If you're starting out right now and that really sounded alien to you, here is one quick paragraph on the basics: First, know that when you lose a trade, it's not personal. The market is not out to get you. It will feel like it but it's not personal. (The only exception is if you trade with a forex or CFD broker that operates a dealing desk business model... then yes, as a former dealer, I can tell you that they may have personally triggered your Stop Loss.) In general: no, the market does not care about you. It's just that difficult to do successfully, and even if/when you eventually do it well, you will still have to accept losing trades. You'll just have the positive EV to overcome the losing trades. As for trading psychology? Honestly, it depends on your personality. For some, it feels like psychology is overblown by trading educators and not as big of a deal as it's made out to be. For others, it'll be the key to staying profitable without self sabotage. Either way, there's more than enough literature about that topic, mostly written by people who have never had a single profitable year in a live trading account, so let's move on.

Here's what others don't usually tell you:

Other people's ideas and beliefs about risk management may not apply to you and your style of trading.

Many people - including those who only learned to trade recently - tend to state certain principles as if they were universal truths. Some of these people are trying to sell you products. Others are well-meaning but simply don't know any better due to their own lack of experience.

Either way, if they tell you to "always" do something or "never" do something in relation to risk management, always consider that it's entirely possible that their beliefs may not apply to your situation.

WHAT BEGINNERS ARE TAUGHT

Most beginners are taught to simply risk a flat percentage (typically 2%, 1%, 0.5%, etc.) of their trading capital per trade.

Static percentage-based risk management methods are helpful to prevent beginners from losing as quickly as if they had over-leveraged, but they're not optimized to take advantage of strategies with a strong positive Expected Value (if you have one.)

The purpose of this method is to prevent runs of losses from causing undue damage to the account balance while capitalizing on runs of wins. For that, this type of rule theoretically does its job.

One of the problems with the static percentage per trade rule, and similar sizing methods, is that every single losing trade will reduce your balance, no matter how small, and necessarily reduce your next winning trade's size. In effect, inevitable short runs of losing trades would cause your next winning trade to be less potent in regaining those losses.

For example, if you began with a $1000 balance and

you size your trade such that you risk $20 (which is 2% of $1000) on your first trade and you lose, your balance has been reduced to $980. On your next trade, a 2% risk (of $980) would dictate that you would only be risking $19.60. Assuming your strategy's edge hasn't changed, your potential win has also been reduced by 2% even though the new trade's potential is just as valid as the last.

The rationale behind the 2% risk per trade method was grounded in the fact that risking small percentages per trade can effectively slow the shrinkage of an account balance even if you trade with a losing strategy.

The same technique can be applied to negative-edge games of chance like a slot machine or casino roulette - where you'll still lose by the laws of nature if you repeatedly participate, you'll simply lose much slower than someone betting their entire bankroll on each wager.

If you do a little research on "betting systems" being sold to gamblers who play casino games (with a built-in negative edge for the player), you'll find the same 2% rule taught for "bankroll size." In fact, some of those systems are created by the same types of online marketers who only recently discovered that the trading niche is a profitable online marketing niche, and they quickly teach this type of risk management because they just read it a few days before creating their own courses and products.

The flat percentage per trade risk method is designed to be a way for net losers to lose slowly.

Winners can still use it successfully - many have done so - but there are better ways to capitalize on a positive EV than a method designed to keep negative EV players active.

When you're trading a prop firm challenge account, it does make sense to reduce your exposure to inevitable losing streaks, but there are much better ways to do it than a static percentage risk.

PROBABILITIES OF WINNING TRADES

You don't need a degree in statistics for this section. You don't even have to be inherently good at math beyond some very basic third-grade level math, at most.

People will give you the well-meaning advice, "Always trade with risk-reward higher than 1R," meaning you always go for profit targets that are at least 1 x Risk (1R) or higher. So, if you place a trade that risks $10, they are telling you that you absolutely must target $10 or more - preferably $20 or more. Their logic, as traditionally preached by trading educators, is that it takes less than a 50% win rate to be profitable if you always trade with a 2R or better risk-reward ratio.

In theory, that's true.

The piece of the puzzle they are missing (or are ignorant of) is that win rate is inherently inverse to risk-reward. With all else being equal, it's half as likely for the market to move $20 away than it is to move $10 away. (This is not universally true, depending on the nature of your strategy, but if you randomly enter at any given time, this is the case. And it makes no sense to stack the odds against yourself from the start.)

In inverse, therefore, is also true. If you trade with 0.5R then you are twice as likely to hit your target.

The following table shows the minimum win rates needed to maintain positive EV with a given ratio of risk (loss size) to reward (win size).

	WinRate	WinSize	LossSize	EV
Strategy A: 3R	26.0%	3	1	+0.04
Strategy B: 2R	34.0%	2	1	+0.02
Strategy C: 1R	51.0%	1	1	+0.02
Strategy D: 0.5R	67.0%	1	2	+0.01
Strategy E: 0.33R	76.0%	1	3	+0.04

The following shows what happens with the same risk-reward ratios when your win rate drops.

	WinRate	WinSize	LossSize	EV
Strategy A: 3R	24.0%	3	1	-0.04
Strategy B: 2R	33.0%	2	1	-0.01
Strategy C: 1R	49.0%	1	1	-0.02
Strategy D: 0.5R	66.0%	1	2	-0.02
Strategy E: 0.33R	74.0%	1	3	-0.04

The oldest argument in favor of "always" having a high risk-reward (large profit targets and small stop losses) is because of this. It doesn't take a high win rate to achieve profitability with that kind of risk-reward.

However, in reality, some trading styles need more room to breathe and not every market environment hands out large profit targets without first touching the nearby stop loss.

Recall that, all else being equal, it is twice as likely for the market to move 10 points in either direction than it is to move 20.

Most trading strategies attempt to pinpoint the situations where this is possible. However, consider for a second that most trading educators who advocate for those styles are not actually profitable traders (most make their money from YouTube ad revenue, courses, etc.) And most retail traders who believe in those styles are also not profitable.

If you trade one of those styles and you're already making money with it, you can go ahead and continue using it. You found your positive EV.

For everyone else, who has struggled to replicate the results of people who preach those ideas, but really want to try to pass a prop firm evaluation and then trade profitably enough to withdraw profits, then it might be a good idea to consider something different.

	WinRate	WinSize	LossSize	EV
Strategy A: 3R+	24.0%	3.2	1	+0.01
Strategy B: 2R+	33.0%	2.1	1	+0.02
Strategy C: 1R+	49.0%	1.1	1	+0.03
Strategy D: 0.5R+	66.0%	1.1	2	+0.05
Strategy E: 0.33R+	74.0%	1.1	3	+0.03

Notice that in this table, the win rates are the same as the one before (the one with the negative EV results.) All this did was increase the win size by a little while retaining the loss sizes.

If you take your favorite trading strategy, and modify it so that you give your trades more room to breathe, you might be surprised at how much more often you will win. (This assumes you have a decent strategy, of course. If you learned a strategy that's based on moon cycles and flipping coins, it might be disappointing... but, even then, your win rate will still be higher than if you trade that same strategy with overly tight stop losses.)

To be clear, I am not advocating only for small risk-reward ratios universally. I'm trying to clarify that high risk-reward trading styles - as often taught by others who are not actually profitable traders themselves as the only option - is not a prerequisite for a strategy to be profitable. It's only one of many ways a strategy can be profitable. And they are the least comfortable ways to trade.

Most of the material emphasizing psychology also happens to be the same sources who treat that type of low win rate strategy. Of course it's psychologically difficult to trade a strategy that loses two-thirds of the time.

Either you have high risk-reward or you have a high win rate. Inherently, it's difficult to achieve both. The purpose of specific strategies is to find the situations where you can push both in your favor just enough to achieve a positive Expected Value.

This does not mean that you are risking larger amounts per trade. One of the benefits of trading with a prop firm is that you aren't restricted by your own amount of capital. You're not forced to trade instruments with minimum tick sizes that are too large for your account balance. Even in the smallest prop accounts of 5000 to 10,000 starting balances, you can still trade multiple Micro futures contracts or multiple micro lots in forex. This allows your larger stop losses to simply equate to an appropriately smaller trade size.

It's simply not as black-and-white as most beginners are taught.

APPROACHES TO ACCOUNT RISK

Some people will use blanket statements like, "Always add to winners." That's often true... for certain types of strategies. It depends on the nature of your strategy and your core style of trading. It's not as universal as some people make it appear to be.

In general, it's a good rule of thumb to cut your losses and let your winners run. It's a well-meaning generalization that applies to most beginners, especially if you tend to not admit you're wrong and let a losing trade turn into an enormous loss. It's also because beginners are almost exclusively taught trading styles that rely on this type of risk management.

Every time I see people preach "always" use stop

losses and then regurgitate a quote from Warren Buffett to reinforce their own ideas, I just see unintentional irony. Warren Buffett does not use stop losses. He doesn't have to because he trades (yes, long-term investment is a trading style) in a way that does not require it. He also has a very large base of capital and a very high win rate. Most people who idolize him are not in the same boat... but it doesn't mean everyone else must universally abide by rigid, dogmatic self-imposed rules.

The problem is that all of those "always" and "never" statements, when believed, create a very inflexible way of looking at risk management.

It's difficult to abide by those types of "always/never" rules without unintentionally causing your trading style to become extremely rigid and limited. This type of mindset is not great for adapting to different market conditions.

Instead, consider the following:

A Large Capital Large/No Stops	B Large Capital Small Stops
C Small Capital Large/No Stops	D Small Capital Small Stops

A: Large Capital with Large/No Stops. If you happen to be starting with millions in capital, this can work if you're trading a very small percentage of your capital per trade. Since you have a large amount of capital, it also means those relatively small percentages you make will still be a good amount of money, so it won't be difficult to do this.

B: Large Capital with Small Stops. You may not always be the top-performing fund in the world, but you'll have a better chance at making a good living, knowing you are very unlikely to wipe out a year's worth of gains with only one losing trade.

C: Small Capital with Large/No Stops. Most beginners love to try this way of trading. It can be done if you also trade using a very small percentage of your capital (for example: if you trade forex at OANDA, you can size your trades down to single units of currency.) The challenge is that every winning trade will be a very small absolute amount of money. Waiting weeks or months for $10 is psychologically challenging to maintain. The temptation to add size to this type of approach is the real risk. And if you add size without reducing the maximum loss per trade, a single losing trade can be catastrophic.

D: Small Capital with Small Stops. This is how most retail traders are taught to trade. It's not wrong but it can also be extremely psychologically challenging for beginners who are not accustomed to admitting that they were wrong - frequently and without hesitation. If you trade with manual stops, you will find it difficult to pull the trigger when you have to take the small losses that make this type of approach work. If you trade with actual stop loss orders, you will be tempted to move the stop and you will also have the added risk that your broker can see your stop orders (this is a real concern if you are trading with a retail forex broker or CFD broker.)

Risk management is a balancing act. Not every type of strategy is alike.

Momentum strategies work best with B or D.

Mean reversion strategies are more likely to need A or C to survive but can potentially be done with B or D.

Carry trades, income, and other long-term strategies almost always require A or C to work.

Regardless of which approach you apply, there is one reality you cannot avoid: You will lose sometimes.

The only requirement is that you have a safety net that prevents a single losing trade from giving you a loss that's unacceptable for your risk tolerance (and for the size of your loss limits under a prop firm.)

While it may seem difficult to trade a style that fits under A or C within the loss limits of a prop firm, it still may be feasible if it's the style you trade. Just be sure you choose sizes that allow for the drawdowns you may face (make use of Micro contracts in futures or smaller lot sizes in forex) to avoid hitting your loss limit in a few trades.

This is generally not a recommended way to trade unless you have millions in your own capital that you're willing to lose. The reason this is mentioned here is because it may be helpful to keep your mind open to ways of adapting such an approach into something with its own loss limits (less than the evaluation account's loss limits, of course) which result in a less rigid stop loss technique than the way most beginners are taught.

Depending on the rules of your prop firm, it may be possible to adapt some of the ideas from these styles of account risk to work within the rules.

CHAPTER 5
TRADE SIZING TO PASS

Trade sizing is often combined with risk management, which it arguably is a major part of. However, trade sizing is such an important part of succeeding or failing at passing prop firm evaluations, that I felt it deserves its own chapter in this book.

Before we move on to the core of this chapter, it's important to cover some of the ways you **should not** attempt to pass evaluations.

DO NOT RUSH IT (TOO MUCH)

Don't be tempted to try to pass a prop firm evaluation in one trade, even if it's allowed.

Firstly, most prop firms will not allow you to do this. There is typically a consistency rule that says a single trade cannot be more than a percentage of your total profit when you hit the profit target. That percentage may be anywhere from 25% to 50% at some firms. Either way, no prop firm wants a trader who gambles the entire maximum loss limit on a single trade.

While some people blame this on the prop firm's desire to prevent traders from passing evaluation, it's objectively a fair rule even if that weren't the reason. (That's not to say that the company isn't benefiting from failed evaluations, only that the rule is valid otherwise.) Whether you trade with your own money, investors' money, or a prop firm's money, a real trader never gambles an entire monthly loss limit on a single trade.

The desire for instant gratification is a dangerous thing in any business. And the only way to "get rich quick" in trading is to risk "going broke quicker."

I fully understand the desire to pass your evaluation challenge as soon as possible, so you can move on to trading for potential withdrawals of profits. Failing costs money so you should factor that into your risks.

MARTINGALE & GAMBLER'S FALLACY

Some traders will read "Martingale" and immediately dismiss it. They're not entirely wrong, but it's included here to illustrate a dangerous concept based on a logical fallacy and to open your mind to ways you can take inspiration from it to create a safer alternative from pieces of the concept behind it.

Martingale is an old technique that doubles the next size following each loss. As the theory goes, every loss can be covered by the next winner. Unfortunately, long runs of losses happen to everyone - even the best traders in the world have them. And runs of losses can last longer than you estimate, even if you have a winning strategy.

Martingale is inherently based on gambler's fallacy - the belief that luck "must" turn around after an arbitrary run of losses. No, it really doesn't. That kind of thinking will only be efficient at one thing: making your capital shrink as fast as possible. Generally, if a trader relies on Martingale in order to be profitable, it's simply because the trader is not very skilled and does not have a positive EV.

As a professional trader, it's important to see past these kinds of logical fallacies. However, Martingale is presented here as an objective view of a flawed concept that might inspire a safe alternative.

LIMITED MARTINGALE - ADVANCED

The only variant of Martingale that can potentially work for some traders is a limited version. For example, if your trading style tends to need some room to breathe, you can plan ahead by starting with one-third of your full trade size, and after the next reversal, you can enter another two-thirds. This has the effect of increasing your probability of winning trades while also not amplifying your losses to a dangerous degree.

As with all risk management methods, you must weigh the benefits and drawbacks of this in relation to your trading strategy. Firstly, consider whether it would be better to simply wait to enter your trade where you normally would have entered your second portion. The tradeoff, however, is that you might miss some of the trades from your normal entry. So, this is not universally better than a Limited Martingale, because there are strategies that might benefit from having some smaller partial profits from the normal entry style.

Also, if you have a personality that makes it difficult to accept losses, it may be worth reconsidering if this style of trading would work for you, because it may tempt you to add to losing trades.

PROP FIRM MAX LOSS SIZING

When trading prop firm evaluations, the optimal risk management method is achieved by dividing the maximum loss limit. For example, at the beginning of the month, you know that there are approximately 25 trading days in a month.

Risk per Trade =
Max Loss / Days to Renewal / # Daily Trades

Max Loss: The remaining maximum loss limit for your account. Keep in mind this may be trailing for most prop firm accounts. (Meaning: it may be the max loss from the peak unrealized profit you last reached instead of the original max loss.)

Days to Renewal: The number of trading days remaining before the evaluation renewal date.

 # Daily Trades: The number of trades you usually take per day.

So, if your maximum loss limit is $5000, you divide it by 25, which gives you $200 per day. If your strategy trades twice per day, you can divide $200 by 2 and your risk per trade should be $100.

This is effectively a "monthly max loss" risk management method, whether you trade for a prop firm or if you trade your own funds this way.

Using this method, you can then calculate the actual number of contracts traded.

Position Size =
(Risk per Trade) / (Stop Size x Point Value)

Risk per Trade: The dollar amount to risk on each trade (from above.)

Stop Size: The size of the trade's stop loss. (For example, if it's 10 points on the Micro ES, then this is 10.00)

Point Value: The value per point of the instrument. (For the Micro ES futures contract, this would be $5 per point. For forex, this would be

100,000 per lot or 1,000 per micro lot.)

So, using the numbers from the previous example for Risk per Trade, if your Risk per Trade was found to be $100, and you are trading the Micro ES futures contract with a 10.00 point stop loss, then:

Risk per Trade = $100
Stop Size = 10
Point Value = 5.00

Position Size = 100 / (10 x 5)
Position Size = 100 / 50
Position Size = 2

In this example, you would trade up to a maximum of 2 Micro ES contracts per trade.

As long as you have a positive EV, this method will increase your probability of passing your prop firm evaluation challenges as fast as possible.

Normally, it sounds good to advocate for traders to trade the same way whether you are trading a prop firm evaluation account or your own money... but that's simply not true.

If you had a college athletes' tryout where you had a limited time (or you had to pay college tuition again to retry - equivalent to a monthly renewal) to prove your ability, there are things you may have to do during that tryout that might be faster or more abbreviated than the way you would perform in a real game. Even if the tryout is designed in a well-meaning way to maximize the simulation of a real game, it's still not the real game.

You know the rules of the game, and you understand that there are specific circumstances that might mean the difference between being drafted into a professional league or forever remaining an amateur.

Thankfully, in trading, the stakes are not quite that extreme and the cost of a monthly renewal is not in the realm of student loan debt for a single semester at a school with a famous college team.

If you're close to the next monthly renewal, it makes very little sense to trade with exactly the same risk sizing as you did at the beginning of the month... unless, of course, your prop firm's rules are ridiculously restrictive about consistent sizing. (You should check the rules of the firm you trade with before implementing the ideas here to avoid inadvertently breaking one.)

As long as the size of your trades, your profits, and your losses per trade stay within the parameters of the rules at your chosen prop firm, this is the approach you should take to optimize your time and effort in the evaluation phase.

Trading is a business. This is true whether you trade your own accounts or you trade with other people's money. When you trade for a prop firm, you are legally classified as an independent contractor, not an employee. When you pass an evaluation, you are contracting your services as a trader to the prop firm. So, you are running a business and it's your responsibility to protect the business by learning risk management. Revenge trading would be akin to a movie studio losing 150 million at the box office and then insisting on making an equally expensive sequel without any evidence from the market to indicate that it would be a good idea.

Keep track of what's working and what isn't. If you trade like a compulsive gambler pushing buttons, you'll lose like one, and this industry will be happy to take your donation.

Trade sizing isn't just about limiting losses. If you do it right, it can also be about maximizing your gains and may make the difference between passing or failing a prop firm challenge.

CHAPTER 6
TYPES OF TRADING STRATEGIES

There are two types of directional trading strategies, which are typically allowed in all prop firm accounts.

MOMENTUM

Momentum strategies have been a staple of trading since the early days of trading in the pits. All variants of trend-following strategies belong to this family, even if they're distant cousins.

It's also one of the first types of strategies taught to beginners because it's often seen as, theoretically, less likely to put a beginner on the wrong side of larger moves.

So much so, that some of you will undoubtedly let out a collective sigh at the very sign of yet another introduction to "follow the trend" concepts. "The trend is your friend," and similar advice is already a cliche in retail trading communities.

If you're one of them, you should still find some value in analyzing the thought process behind momentum strategies in ways that you may not have considered before.

As early as Jesse Livermore, and likely for untold generations before him, the most observant of traders have noticed that a simple tendency of human behavior has always pushed markets in one direction longer than something more rational ever would.

Fortunately for traders, all it takes for these types of strategies to retain their potential is for human irrationality (including the computers programmed by humans to exploit that same irrationality) to continue to exist and trade in the same way. For all the progress we've made as a species in other areas, humans continue to react the same way to new high prices and new low prices. It doesn't even matter if those prices are in a financial market, on Amazon, or at a brick-and-mortar store.

So, momentum strategies remain a reliable part of a professional trader's arsenal.

Moving average trend trading, range breakouts, the infamous Turtle system, and countless others are some of the most well-known momentum strategies in the world. They're not necessarily the optimal methods of exploiting momentum in the markets, but they still have potential in certain contexts. (Many of these strategies have failed on some timeframes but continue to survive in other timeframes. If you are able to backtest them, be sure to stay open to trying different timeframes. You might be surprised to find that a strategy you dismissed years ago can still be profitable there.)

Academics have long believed that markets are a "random walk," so to speak. In the Efficient Market Hypothesis, every known material fact has already been priced into the market, so there's theoretically no way to consistently extract profits from the markets. A major part of the academic world has operated under the assumption that the efficient market hypothesis is true for years - though, in recent years, many have come to accept a less extreme iteration of the theory in the face of evidence to the contrary. If you're interested in the academic side of this, there are a few papers you can find on the internet showing the effect of momentum and "long tail distributions," which traders consider to be trending markets.

There are other reasons that momentum strategies remain, to this day, one of the most commonly taught concepts in the trading world. It's also one of the only families of strategies that won't cannibalize much of its own edge by being shared and taught to others. In fact, there are cases where some momentum strategies can be enhanced.

You may have noticed that the strategies most vendors teach to beginners are likely to get you into a momentum trade far too late. In some cases, it really may be their attempt to balance between getting in too early (catching a falling knife by entering before the previous trend ends) or too late. In other cases, the person teaching you may extract some benefits from being able to front-run those who follow their methods.

Most momentum strategies rely on systematically taking proportionately smaller losses in hopes of catching the largest waves of movement.

This is an inherent part of trading momentum. You absolutely must be able to take frequent, small losses when you are wrong.

A basic range breakout trade looks wonderful on paper, but what most people don't teach beginners is that these types of moves tend to happen less than 40% of the time (depending on which timeframe you trade.) You have to overcome to low win rate with a positive risk-reward (relation between average win size and average loss size.)

Recall that win rate, win size, and loss size are all critical parts of the positive EV recipe.

This is where momentum strategies taught to beginners are double-edged swords. It's the least harmful type of strategy for beginners to learn because it doesn't diminish the teacher's edge much (if they ever had one) and it's not likely to put the beginner on the wrong side of a trend. Yet it's the most difficult to execute because of the strict risk management required for momentum strategies to maintain positive EV.

Most of the often-repeated types of advice you'll find in trading communities tend to be applicable exclusively to momentum strategies.

Things like "never add to losing trades" and "always cut your losses and let your winners run" are great advice for momentum traders. They do not apply to other strategies.

However, it shouldn't be about exclusively picking and choosing. You should develop at least one of each type of strategy to be part of your trading arsenal, so you can thrive in different market conditions.

MEAN REVERSION

The other side of the coin from Momentum is the category of Mean Reversion strategies. These are counter-trend approaches, but not necessarily against the trend on every timeframe - only the one you are mainly watching.

The premise behind the Mean Reversion family is the tendency for markets to over-extend and revert back to an average.

If you're a day trader, you'll find that trend-following Momentum strategies work best in the first 2 hours after major markets open (the opening hour beginning 08:00 in London for GBP/USD and the FTSE index, or 9:35am in New York for US indices like the S&P500, NASDAQ, and Dow Jones Industrial Index). They won't work that well at other times of day.

This is where Mean Reversion strategies shine.

The most basic example of a Mean Reversion strategy is to look for bounces off the previous day's high or low, or a previous trading session's high or low. Don't just blindly take these reversal trades, of course. But if you see the market struggle to break through those levels, trading in the opposite direction can offer great risk-reward and probability.

There are more complex variations of this approach, and variations on different timeframes (by watching weekly highs and lows, for example) but the idea is the same.

Additionally, any strategy that is predicated on the idea that a market has moved to an over-extended point - and is primed for a reversal - also belongs to this family. It's important not to be fooled by the illusion that a strong trending move is an over-extended move. The old saying goes that markets can remain irrational longer than you can remain solvent. Don't assume every time it "looks" over-extended, it will reverse soon. Instead, look for times and prices that show signs of failure to break through.

Depending on your style, this family of strategies can be equally reliant on tight stop losses, but this is not as universal as it is for trend-following strategies. In fact, some Mean Reversion strategies used by institutions allow for a lot more room. The balance you have to maintain is the ability to stay within your prop firm's maximum loss limits while also making the profitable trades worth your time and effort.

Understand that the mean reversion category is naturally the opposite of the momentum family.

Momentum strategies rely on the "fat tails" of price behavior - that is, they profit from the unusually large movements away from the average and can only survive when such divergences exist. Those large divergences are the bread and butter of momentum traders. When a market wildly moves in either direction, a seasoned momentum trader, who has likely endured a long period of taking small losses over and over, finally gets to take home the bacon in the form of a giant payoff.

Meanwhile, on the opposite side of the same events, the mean reversion traders who were making a steady income for all that time will suddenly experience losses.

How can a professional trader possibly choose which approach to follow? The answer is not to choose one or the other.

Don't let others in the trading communities force you into one type of strategy or the other. Keep an open mind and try different approaches to the market. At best, you should have at least one or more Momentum strategies, as well as one or more Mean Reversion strategies, so you are prepared to take on any type of market condition.

The only real requirement is that the strategies you employ from these two categories aren't playing opposite sides of the same underlying market. They can play two sides of correlated markets, but preferably not the exact same one. And it's rare for that to happen if you're exploiting an edge in both categories. Taking opposite trades on the same instrument, even in multiple accounts, may be against the terms of your prop firm. It also shows a lack of skill, which makes your ability to pass the evaluation much less valuable to anyone outside of yourself.

If you have the kind of personality that gravitates toward mean reversion strategies (be it picking bottoms and tops of a market or a ratio between two markets) then learning to run a momentum strategy or two will only be a form of insurance.

Likewise, if you naturally tend to trade momentum methods like breakouts and trend-following approaches - it'd be nice to get paid a little while you're taking all those small losses on your road to the big trending waves.

EV INTO THE FUTURE

Beginners tend to assign far too much significance to the entry and exit method of a strategy. Your strategy is not only how you enter an exit. It's also the size of your trades, the times you trade, and the premise behind the trade.

Diversify the strategies you trade and make it a habit to track your EV for each strategy. It'll help you pass prop firm evaluations and also make you a better trader even if you plan to trade your own capital in the future.

CHAPTER 7
THE PRINCIPLE OF PRICE & TIME

Most traders are taught that markets go up because there is more buying than selling, and they go down when there is more selling than buying. That's part of the picture... but it's missing a few important pieces.

Like many of the most often repeated beliefs in the world, it's not necessarily wrong... but it can paint an incomplete picture of how the real world works.

There are many ways that markets can be manipulated. In small, illiquid markets like penny stocks, they can be manipulated by a single market maker. In larger names, there are usually multiple large market makers and other players who may act like surrogate market makers. In a highly liquid market like forex, the major institutions, whose trading makes up the vast majority of every pair's daily turnover, are the movers of the market. In all of these cases, their actions can only benefit them if there are people to take the other side of their trades.

The most a dealer or market maker can do is advertise a price (post bids and asks, which are just Limit Buy and Limit Sell orders), it's up to participants (such as yourself, but also the hedge funds and other institutions) to agree to those prices.

To illustrate this, let's break it down to the core of what exactly makes a market move up or down. Even if you feel this is extremely basic, it may be worth reviewing this information at a base level so you can truly understand what is happening when a market moves.

First, it's important to understand: What exactly are the bid and ask prices advertising to the public?

THE BEST BID

At any given moment, the **best bid** is the highest that any participant is willing to pay. (It doesn't matter if the person posting the bid is a market maker or another participant, which can happen on centralized exchanges. The bid is still the highest that anyone is willing to pay, so when you place a Market Sell order, that's the highest price you can sell to.) They are Limit Buy orders showing the highest that a seller can get for the asset at this moment.

THE BEST ASK

Likewise, the **best ask** (or offer) is the lowest that any participant is willing to sell (or short sell) for. They are Limit Sell orders. It's the lowest price you can pay if you want to enter as a buyer at this moment.

There are only two reasons the market can ever move in each direction.

WHY A MARKET MOVES UP

1. All Asks (Offers) Are Bought Up:

- Buyers aggressively enter the market by crossing the spread to hit the Ask (offer) with Market Buy orders. Market Buy orders continue buying until they've been matched with all of the selling interest advertised (with Sell Limit orders) at the Ask price.

- **There is volume** because transactions take place.

- If the new best ask is far away, it's easy to notice that **no time was spent at the prices between** the previous best ask and the new best ask.

2. The Best Advertised Ask (Offer) Cancels:

- People advertising the ask price (Sell Limit orders) decide to cancel their Limit Sell orders, so the best ask is now the higher one that was standing in line behind it.

- **No volume is recorded** because no transactions occur. The only change was the order at the front of the line was canceled so the best ask is now the next higher one up.

- **Time is spent at the price** before moving because transactions had to occur.

WHY A MARKET MOVES DOWN

1. All Bids Are Sold to:

- Sellers aggressively enter the market by crossing the spread to hit the best bid with Market Sell orders. Market Sell orders continue selling until they've been matched with all buying interest advertised (with Buy Limit orders) at the bid price.

- **There is volume** because transactions take place.

- If the new best bid is far away, it's easy to notice that **no time was spent at the prices between** the previous best bid and the new best bid.

2. The Best Advertised Bid Moves Down:

- People who advertised their interest in buying at the bid (Limit Buy orders) decide to cancel their Limit Buy orders so the best bid is now the lower Limit Buy orders standing in line behind it.

- **No volume is recorded** because no transactions occur. The only change was the order at the front of the line was canceled so the best bid is now the next lower one down.

- **Time is spent at the price** before moving because transactions had to occur.

So, in both directions, price either moves because all of the **advertised Limit orders are matched** (trades happen) or the **orders at the front of the line are cancelled**.

Both of these events look like "movement" in the market but they are two different events.

The former shows actual interest from the other side of the market. The latter only shows that the front of the line decided to get out of the way, even when there is no interest at all.

The only caveat about time without volume is that time can be an illusion since a bid or offer that attracts no volume can still stay at a price for a while. The key is that lack of time at a price, such as when a market moves far very quickly, correlates well with when there is no real interest in the prices in between. Ideally, having real volume data would be best, which is always available for centralized exchanges as in stocks and futures markets. However, in decentralized markets such as forex, no source of volume data is 100% accurate. (Many of the largest transactions are taking place directly between large banks, who do not report all of their transactions, live and to the public.) Tick volume and futures volume correlates well with real volume, which is good enough for most purposes. Just be aware that no one has 100% accurate volume data for forex.

This may seem overly elementary, but I've been surprised how many traders, who have traded for years, never came to fully understand this basic mechanism behind why markets move.

If it still doesn't feel intuitive to you, here is an analogy from outside of the financial markets:

Imagine three gas stations at the same intersection. Knowing the average price of gasoline was $2.50 the previous week, Station A offers $2.60 per gallon and Station B offers $2.40 per gallon.

Both are busy with customers. That's a lot of volume because the buyers and sellers have come to a consensus where they generally agree that the $2.40 to $2.60 range is an acceptable price range to buy and sell gasoline within. A lot of time is spent in this range.

The third gas station, however, decides to advertise $10 per gallon. Not a single customer goes to buy from that one.

If this were a financial market, it would be showing a lot of volume at $2.60 and $2.40 all day.

Then, if the first two gas stations both close for the day, the best offer would then show $10.

On your chart, you would see a "move" up to $10 because that is now the best ask price... but there is zero volume at $10 because customers would rather wait till the next day to fill up than pay $10 per gallon right now.

Based on volume (actual transactions), you can see that the market has not moved with legitimate demand even though the price chart shows there was a move up to $10.

If, however, the other two gas stations notice that

they are running out of gasoline supplies, and they both start to raise the price to $2.70... then $2.80... and so on, as demand eats up their supply (rising volume as it moves up), then it's easy to notice that each of the levels draw interest on the way up to a top of the range (which likely still won't go straight to $10, though.)

This is why it's important to understand the difference between the two ways that price moves.

Having learned this, you might wonder, "Does that mean I have to learn to use volume to trade?"

You can do that, of course. If you're trading in a centralized market such as stocks or futures, you can use real volume data to understand what is really happening.

If you are trading a decentralized market such as forex, there are no reliable sources of real volume data. However, it has been found that tick volume - which is available from most retail forex platforms - approximates real volume with about 80% correlation. This is imperfect, but if you are a forex trader, it's one of the easier routes to take. Alternatively, if you have access to live futures data, you can use the volume data from the futures contracts on the same currency pairs as a proxy for the actual volume in the spot forex market.

PRICE, TIME, AND PROFILES

If you are a TPO or Market Profile® (a registered

trademark of the CME) trader, you may track the "footprints" of volume on the Y-axis of your chart as a way to find where the real interest was found in recent history. Many traders find this tool to be a great way to discover where clusters of limit orders are likely to be the next time the market returns to those levels.

Why? Because, as in the gas station analogy, imagine if all of the stations had gradually crept up to $3.50 or higher. The next time they all drop their prices down to the $2.50 area, customers in the area are likely to remember that was an old price range, "back when gas was cheaper." In all markets, this measurement of cheap and expensive is arbitrary and based entirely on the memory of the participants in the market.

In financial markets, this is clear in many ways. It tends to manifest itself as a reaction to an old area where the market found a lot of interest, so the participants are also likely to show a lot of interest again the next time the market returns to that area.

This is the basis for every strategy that talks about support, resistance, supply and demand zones, value, psychological levels, or any other term that refers to the same behavioral tendencies - which have been part of every market since the beginning of time.

Does that mean you 100% need TPO or Market Profile® charts? Not really. You can use them if you find that they help you visualize where the areas of interest are... but you can also do it yourself by looking at "zones" where the market has bounced around and spent a lot of time in the recent past.

Remember, the principle behind all of it is the same:

THE UNIVERSAL PRICE-TIME ANALYSIS

The more time that a market spends in a price area, the more interest is shown in that price. The time spent in the area is also highly predictive of the amount of volume transacted within that price area.

After spending many years dealing against traders, then working with traders who use many different styles of analysis - from range breakouts to support and resistance to "smart money" and everything in between - I've found that successful traders are all looking for the same thing.

"At what price ranges did the market spend the most time before?"

Whether each trader realizes it or not, this is what they are looking for when they get good at this game.

For successful technical indicator traders, it's a subconscious (or automated) process that they've developed in relation to some arbitrary signals from indicators caused by this behavior - on purpose or not.

For successful price action traders, it's based on swing highs and swing lows which tend to encompass these areas.

For some old traders, it may just be a method based on an older book or mentor that taught them the habit of looking for these zones as support and resistance areas while they draw diagonal trendlines and channels to trade near the areas.

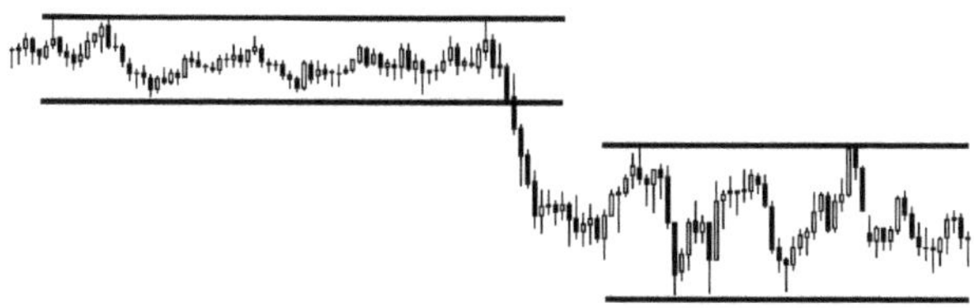

For breakout traders, these are the areas they like to draw lines at the top and bottom of in order to trade when the market breaks away from them.

For mean reversion traders, these are the areas treated as a magnet to which the market is likely to return after a long move away from it.

For profile and TPO traders, these are areas highlighted by the thick parts of the profile tools they are using.

In all of these cases, those who are successful at trading are likely to, in one way or another, end up analyzing data that amounts to identifying the same main source of information: Where did price spend the most time before?

When a market returns to areas where it spent a lot of time in the past, it's more likely to stall there because of the cluster of limit orders sitting in that zone. This means these areas are good potential profit targets (depending on the approach of your strategy) or good areas to trade breakouts away from.

When the market moves away from these areas, there tends to be less opposition to the movements. With all else being equal, you are far more likely to find a buttery smooth move in "open air" areas (where the market spent **less time** in the recent past) than where the market spent a lot of time before.

The more time the market spends in an area, the more participants have **come to a consensus** on the price zone. (This is like the $2.40 to $2.60 range in the gasoline analogy.)

The less time is spent in an area, the more likely you will see larger moves with less opposition. This is like if an Amazon seller tries to sell toilet paper for astronomical prices. If it's advertised for $100, it might have gotten some volume in 2020, but since then, it's more likely to drop fast (without pausing to spend much time - at prices in between - because it won't find a lot of interest even at, say, $50) if the seller wants to find any real buyers. When the seller drops to the range of $5 to $10, it's more likely to spend more time there because they'll be more likely to find willing buyers for packages of toilet paper within the range.

So, price and time is a universal principle.

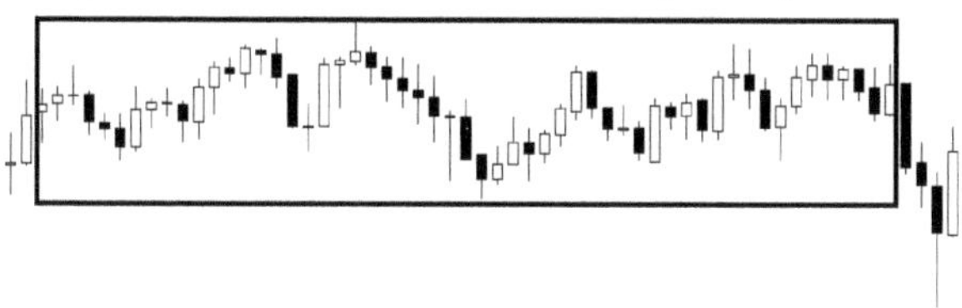

Markets move quickly toward the nearest consensus price area. When finds a consensus area, it spends more time there because transactions take place. If new sentiment pushes the market out of that consensus area, it will move quickly (spend less time at prices) in search of a new consensus area.

Rinse and repeat.

This is how markets behave. It's how markets have always behaved.

It doesn't matter if you believe it's caused by natural market behavioral patterns (which have existed since the first time humans participated in any form of market) or you subscribe to a conspiracy theory about market manipulators and have labeled it some fancy new name for an old concept. You may even have built a complex automated system that exploits parts of this behavior without knowing that's where your edge came from.

Either way, you're still looking at the same thing and seeking to profit from the same behavior.

Once you understand this price-time principle, you will better understand how to search for new opportunities if your old ones are not working under current market conditions.

CHAPTER 8
EXPLOITING TIMES OF DAY

The futures and forex markets are often advertised as 24-hour markets, but that's a bit of a distortion of the truth. It runs for five days straight, from Sunday evening to Friday evening in the east coast of the US, because the hours in each of the major global financial centers (typically 8AM to 5PM in forex, futures exchanges vary) overlap each other. And not all of those hours are likely to be the same. By assuming they are, you will at the very least be bored to death at certain times of day... and shocked into panic at others.

On the most liquid currency pairs and futures contracts, the major financial centers involved are, in order: Sydney, Tokyo, Frankfurt, London, and New York. These cities are also home to the major developed economies, each with equity (stock) markets that open approximately an hour after the banks begin operations for the day. Approximately 8AM to 10AM in each of these cities' respective time zones will typically be the most volatile periods for the major currency pairs. This is especially true for the first hours of operation at the banks in London (8am UK time, which is British Summer Time during Daylight Savings) and New York (the US stock markets open at 9:30am Eastern Time, which is Eastern Daylight Time from March to September.)

The main reason it seems to be so difficult for web sites to get this information entirely right at all times of year is that it's much less straightforward than you would assume at first glance. Firstly, Japan doesn't use Daylight Savings Time, and England has long been considering the end of their use of British Summer Time (their term for Daylight Savings.) Even while England uses it, the dates on which the UK switches to and from BST does not match up with the exact dates when the US switches to and from Daylight Savings. Lastly, Australia also has different Daylight Savings switch dates. And to complicate things further, Australia happens to be in the southern hemisphere, so when everyone else (who uses Daylight Savings at all) is "Springing forward", they're "Falling back" and vice versa, leaving many of the online guides to FX session times inaccurate by an hour for half of the year.

Here's the easiest method to accurately find the start and end times of each financial center's banking hours for forex: Banks in all of these major cities are generally open from 8:00 AM (08:00) to 5:00 PM (17:00) in the respective city's local time zone. By looking up the current time (as of the current date) of each city at any given time, you can better gauge the actual period of expected volatility breakouts of the day.

For stock exchanges and futures exchanges, you can look up the hours. The biggest one is 9:30am Eastern Time for the NYSE and NASDAQ which impacts most major currency pairs, index futures, and anything that interacts with the US - the largest economy in the world. Next in line would be the UK, opening at 8:00am in UK time (which would be British Summer Time in the summer months, one hour ahead of GMT/UTC.)

Why does any of this matter?

Well, momentum traders should only watch the opening hours of London and New York for the big trending moves that are the most likely to present intraday momentum opportunities. Tokyo and Sydney sessions, as well as most of the rest of the day, are often better suited for mean reversion styles if you are day trading, as those can all be relatively range-bound by comparison.

For part-time traders, an added factor to consider is whether each time zone's peak hours (the first couple of hours of the session) overlap with other obligations. Many part-time traders in North America prefer to specialize in the Sydney and Tokyo sessions for this reason alone, as their opening hours are in the North American evening.

Don't let the time on your trading platform confuse you further. Many retail brokers use varying time zones on their trading platforms, which has resulted in a mess when it comes to identifying a single standard for daily bars or candles on Forex charts. However, the generally accepting beginning and end to a day for forex is the end of the American bank hours at 5:00 PM ET (New York time). This standard is relatively consistent since it's typically the time of rollovers (when interest differentials - between the currencies in a pair - is charged or credited for open positions.) It's also the end of the entire trading week on Friday before the market re-opens on Monday morning Australian time (Sunday afternoon in New York).

Likewise, for US futures contracts, the closing time of the CME is the equivalent, as it also closes briefly each day and closes for the weekend on Friday.

Unfortunately, retail FX charting packages aren't all configured to show this properly so it may be necessary to create custom indicators or other utilities to show the actual daily highs and lows.

Most futures platforms show the local time zone by default, but it's worth double-checking this yourself when you first set it up.

As a basis for measuring a currency pair's volatility, you can use Average True Range (ATR) on the daily timeframe. It's a built-in feature on practically every trading platform which calculates the average range (the difference between the high and low) of the timeframe (in this case, daily) and adjusts for gaps between days.

Average True Range is an excellent barometer for market intraday conditions because it allows a trader to gauge the amount of volatility to expect under current market conditions within a reasonable error range. The average taken over a 21-day period is my daily ATR of choice because 21 is the average number of trading days per month. This is generally a large enough sample size to indicate the current volatility environment and at the same time recent enough to be kept up to date at the time of calculation.

Alternatively, you can use the common default of 14 days. The difference shouldn't be too large unless there was a very significant jump in volatility within the last two weeks or so.

The second measure of volatility for intraday traders is the Average First Hour range. Simply subtract the low from the high of the last 21 sessions' local 8AM to 9AM hour to get the Average First Hour. Obviously, it's possible to find the Average First Hour value for four different sessions but the most practical measures are the ones for London's first hour and New York's first hour.

This, unfortunately, is not a standard indicator and may be necessary to manually implement in your trading platform if it provides an API for developing custom indicators.

One or both of these should be more than enough to gauge the current environment from the perspective of intraday forex and futures traders.

As a general rule of thumb, if you expect a lot of volatility, you should trade a trend-following Momentum style of strategy.

If you expect a lower volatility, choppy ranging time of market condition, you should look to trade a Mean Reversion style instead.

If you don't already have your own criteria for your expectations of volatility levels, the most basic guide is the clock.

The first couple of hours in the London session and New York session, for most futures contracts and major currency pairs, should default to Momentum. Other times of day should default to Mean Reversion.

Try not to think in terms of "always" and "never." Instead, think in terms of what is most likely to happen, and when the market shows evidence to confirm that likelihood, you can react appropriately.

CHAPTER 9
UNDERSTANDING PRICE ACTION

A major part of becoming a professional day trader is the ability to read the language of the markets. This is a language spoken through the footprints left behind by price action, volume information, waves of fear and greed, and the collective sentiment of market participants. As a day trader, your primary task is to become fluent in this language, to read between the lines of price action, and to use this understanding to make informed trading decisions.

People who label themselves "pure price action traders" often look down on other forms of trading such as relying on "lagging indicators" because all mathematically calculated indicators - from the standard moving average to a more advanced low pass filter and even volume-based indicators like profiles and VWAP - are all based on past data. That's true. However, all price action that you read on a chart is also the recent past. Even if you only read a tick chart or you're tape reading on the Time & Sales, you're still only able to see movements that happened in the recent past, even if that may be milliseconds ago. And that's okay.

The important part is to understand that your job is not to predict the future with certainty. When you're wrong, you're not necessarily doing your job poorly.

Every time you read price action, you are looking for footprints from the recent past in order to trade the probabilities of the near future. That is your goal.

You are looking for where the price is able to move to... and the areas where it attempts to move but is unable (fails) to continue.

This is why it's important to understand **why** the market moves up or down. If you are not clear on this part, you should review the chapter on the principle of price & time until it feels intuitive to you.

Over time, as a day trader, all you need is to be correct often enough - relative to your average size of winning and losing trades - to achieve positive expectancy. In other words, you only need a win rate high enough that when you put it into the EV formula with your average win size and average loss size, you get a positive number. That is your job.

If you trade at random times without any rational criteria, then you can either attempt to trade with larger stop losses (for larger average losing trades vs winning trades) for a higher win rate with weaker risk-reward, or you can attempt to trade with larger profit targets (for larger average winning trades vs losing trades) for a lower default win rate with stronger risk-reward. With random entries, both should give you approximately breakeven results (minus the cost of spreads and any commissions) over time.

The purpose of choosing entries and exits that are non-random is to give yourself an edge over a coin flip.

You do not have to be correct 100% of the time. No one in the world is. When traders claim to have 90% or higher win rates, they are either lying or they are using the high win rate with weaker risk-reward method above. In the short term, they will create the illusion of accuracy... until the one large losing trade wipes all of it (and more) out.

You only need positive EV. That can be achieve with high win rate or with strong risk-reward. It's a balancing act between risk-reward and win rate. However, also know that it's far more psychologically challenging to consistently execute your plan if you have a low win rate, so the goal is to at least maximize your accuracy within the confines of your ability and the market conditions.

It's not as black and white as most trading educators attempt to frame it.

Why is this being addressed here? Because I know a large percentage of readers will come straight to this chapter, believing entries and exits are all that matter. If that's you, it's entirely understandable. Just bear in mind that the real meat of what will determine your success as a trader is in the other chapters.

Price action is like trying to shoot the ball toward the basket in a game of basketball. You won't win the game if your entire team's plan consists of always running straight toward the basket with no concept of how to dribble, how opponents play, the difference between a layup and a 3-pointer, and how to play defense.

So, if you skipped straight to this chapter - ignoring everything else in this book - you are trying to play basketball by running straight toward the basket, attempting to score in the most predictable way possible.

WHAT IS PRICE ACTION

When most traders talk about price action, they are referring to the idea of trading without technical indicators such as MACD, RSI, Stochastics, etc.

The truth is that there is nothing inherently wrong with those indicators. Granted, they are arguably outdated (much more complex calculations are used in modern algorithmic trading), lagged (due to being calculated from past prices - but price action trading is also based on past prices, which is not a bad thing by itself), and simply unnecessary for many successful traders.

This is all to say that if you happen to trade a style that uses technical indicators and it works for your situation, the markets you trade, and your personality, then there's no reason to stop. Just understand that it's likely that your indicators derive their information from the same principles that are taught by others who do not use any indicators.

Likewise, if you are a "pure price action" trader who does not use any technical indicators, there's no reason to look down on those who do. I know this was likely taught to you by vendors who push the idea of "pure price action" or "naked" trading as the reason for profitability but it's not. It just means that you've learned a style that uses the same principles I explain in this book using an analysis method that doesn't require as many squiggly lines on your screen as others do. So, if one style feels like your "native language" of the markets for you, then continue trading it. It does not inherently make you better or worse than other traders who trade a different style.

Price action is about finding areas of **highs** (where price has **moved upward and bounced off a high** to begin moving downward) and **lows** (where price has **moved downward and bounced off a low** to begin moving upward.)

Examples of this are inevitably going to feel cherry-picked, especially because every example must be in hindsight. Live price action will feel much less "certain." Be aware of that, especially if you are a beginner.

As a trader, you should never expect any analysis to

feel certain, even when you look at the examples in this book. Instead, the purpose is to understand the concept of a bounce off a high or low in price action - even when it looks messy and confusing.

A REVIEW OF THE BASICS

This will be a review of how to read past price action. If you're not a beginner, this may feel tedious and unnecessary, but the purpose is mainly to allow beginners to catch up. If you're still struggling as a trader, it may be helpful to review this either way.

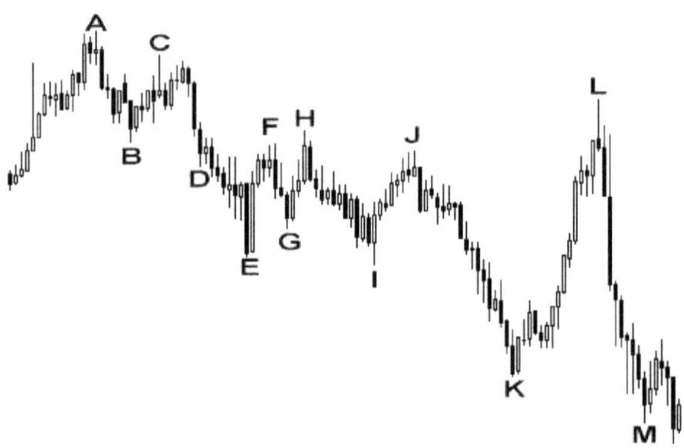

Price Action Example 1

This example is to illustrate the basic "grammar" of reading price action in any market. While an initial glance at this chart may look confusing and messy, the time and price where specific swing highs and swing lows (movements that ended and reversed) are objective.

In an upward movement (uptrend on a lower timeframe), the **peak of a swing high** is where the market reached, **failed to continue higher**, and reversed downward. For example, "A" in Price Action Example 1.

In a downward movement (downtrend on a lower timeframe), the **peak of a swing low** is where the market reached, **failed to continue lower**, and reversed upward. For example, "B" in Price Action Example 1.

In this example, "C" is much "messier" in the sense that it's a failed attempt to seek consensus above and led to a quick drop back into a less extreme upward move. This is usually taught as a pin bar or inverted hammer. What it shows in this context is that the market advertised a fast rise, and other participants didn't agree yet. It took another four candles (this is a 5-minute timeframe chart so that's 20 minutes later) before other participants came closer to the same consensus.

In reality, movements like this can happen for many reasons, but that's less important than understanding that it simply means, in the short term, other participants did not reach a consensus at a higher price than the peak.

If you were selling buttons on Etsy, this would be the equivalent of selling a bunch of buttons at $10 but when you attempt to raise it to $11, you only sold one button but received no more orders. In order to continue making transactions, you'll have to move your ask down to $10 again. And if it still fails to sell more buttons, you may have to consider moving your ask down to $9, and so on. That peak at $11 on your Etsy buttons was the peak of the swing high.

This is a normal part of natural market behavior that's moved in this way long before computers were invented. As a price action trader, you are simply reading the footprints of this behavior.

After "C", you can see that the market failed to break to a higher high (any price higher than the peak at "A"). In other words, there was not enough buying interest to find a consensus at a higher price, even four bars after the first attempt upward at "C", so the sellers who want to participate are becoming a little more desperate - lowering the prices they are willing to sell at.

Naturally, the market would then move on to test the lows instead.

This is a common behavior pattern you will find in all timeframes. A wave of buying (upward) pressure, followed by a wave of selling (downward) pressure, then repeat.

The difference between an uptrend and a downtrend is that, **in an uptrend**, those waves of upward pressure tend to **peak higher** while waves of downward pressure **fail to peak lower**.

Conversely, **in a downtrend**, the waves of downward pressure will **peak lower** while waves of upwardward pressure will **fail to peak higher**.

This is why trends are defined as higher highs and higher lows (for uptrends) or lower lowers and lower highs (for downtrends.)

To summarize trend behavior:

When there is an **upward imbalance** (more buying interest than selling interest), you will see **higher highs** and **higher lows**. This is an **uptrend**.

When there is a **downward imbalance** (more selling interest than buying interest), you will see **lower highs** and **lower lows**. This is a **downtrend**.

As trends weaken, there will be more time spent in a range. Candles will overlap more. (In a strong trend, in either direction, candles will rarely overlap.)

This relation between price and time is what most technical indicators are measuring. The problem is that in a strong trend, this type of weakening behavior can later resume into another strong continuing trending move. This is why many people will dismiss all technical indicators - they will feel like the indicator is "wrong" when it shows a peak that turns out not to be the end of a trending move. The same error can be made in pure price action reading.

This is like if your button-selling Etsy shop suddenly finds a lot of buyers at $9, so you raise the price again to $10. And as the buyers are still frequently coming in, you test $11 again. This time, there are lots of buyers at $11, so you then decide to raise your price to $12, and so on. Your Etsy buttons didn't change, but due to some external factor (maybe an influencer showed off one of your buttons to their 2 million followers), you are now in an uptrend on your Etsy buttons so you can continue raising the price until you find the end of the consensus price range.

Your previous assessment was not wrong. You lowered the price of your Etsy buttons because you didn't find enough buying interest at $11... at the time. Now, due to the market's new sentiment, you are finding buyers much higher than you had earlier.

The technical indicators and price action readers looking at your Etsy prices were not wrong at the time, they simply reported on what had happened until then.

This is why it's important to react rather than to predict when trading, whether you read "pure price action" or 5 technical indicators.

Back to Price Action Example 1: At point "D" in this example, the market has reversed into a downtrend by breaking the previous low. (This also forms a variant of a "head and shoulders" pattern used by some technical analysts, but it's not necessary to memorize most patterns. Just understand the principle of higher highs and higher lows for up, lower highs and lower lows for down.)

At "E", the market exhausts the initial move down and starts to find a new range of consensus.

"F", "H", and "J" are both retests of the top of the consensus range, which is also the bottom of the previous consensus range that "B" bounced off earlier. Notice these are not perfectly horizontal at once specific price. In a real market, you'll see this kind of messiness, where the market is able to break through a little and then quickly falls backward. This is the nature of advertising prices at new highs or lows to test for interest.

Price can be messy because humans (and algorithms programmed by humans) are not always concerned with exact prices. It's the equivalent of getting a lot of buy orders on your Etsy buttons when you move back to $11.50. It's not exactly $11 or exactly $12, but the buyers who were interested within that zone will buy.

"G" and "I" re-test the bottom of the new consensus range established by the exhausted initial move down at "E" earlier.

Most books will show you clean, safe-looking trends that move in one direction. The purpose of this example is to show the opposite - messy, realistic price action that happened.

Looking at "K" in the example, if you pretend you can't see the right side yet, you might think it would be the next move down to a lower consensus range in a gradual downtrend. That's the way most vendors like to teach because it creates an illusion of competence for beginners. (That's good for their sales but not good for beginner traders.)

Reality will confront you with surprises.

After "K", you might expect a bounce below "L"... but "L" shows the market blew past the low of the previous range (there was no longer a lot of selling interest near the bottom established by "E", "G", and "I") and continued up to re-test the prior range high (previously established by "F", "H", and "J") instead.

Likewise, "M" continues this expansion of volatility by blowing past the previous areas in between and landing at the low previously established by "K."

"M" is even lower, which gives the trader a clue about the lack of buying interest to support the market at the bottom of the present range. The right edge of this example shows that the following price action did, in fact, continue further down.

This type of volatility expansion is most common when a major financial center's session opens. (Economic news releases often do it too but tend to move even faster than the movement shown in this example. It would likely be one long candle instead of the "stair step" moves shown in this example if it were caused by a surprising result from a news release.)

What's important to learn from this is that not every break of a previous swing high/low is necessarily a change of trend. It can be an expansion of the range. For most beginners, the better course of action on this type of move is to accept a small loss and wait for the next opportunity.

Price Action Example 2

In Price Action Example 2, "A" establishes a major low followed by a volatility expansion similar to the ending of the previous example.

While these bounces establish a wide range, notice that there isn't a strong consensus, except for the middle of the range, which holds for a little with a **series of overlapping candles** (consensus between buyers and sellers) before a strong break downward. "B" and "C" reinforce that "A" was a strong support area that became a resistance area.

In the Etsy buttons analogy, this would be a scenario after the buying frenzy had ended and you had to lower your price to $8. When a smaller buying trend came in, you were able to raise it to $9 and then $10 again. Then, seeing you sell your buttons for $10, other sellers of similar buttons saw an opportunity and began selling buttons at $10 too. If they charted your prices, they may even notice that $10 was a low you bounced off after the influencer gave you a boost before. They may be in a different situation. They don't want to sell lower than the lowest you sold for during the buying frenzy. So they are posting their buttons on Etsy for $10 but no less than $10. So, now, you can increase your sales volume by offering lower than $10 but you can't offer higher and expect any volume because the other sellers are stacked at $10 and all of your customers on Etsy can see that.

Because financial markets are continuous dual auctions (like a two-sided eBay auction that never ends), a lot of these situations will happen. The important part is to realize that many sellers will see the return to a broken historical low (support) as a good high price to sell now (making it a new resistance.) On the flip side, a previously broken high (resistance) will look like a good cheap price for buyers to buy (making it a new support.)

After breaking to the upside, "D" shows that the same support-turned-resistance level once again becomes a support level for a short time.

Ranges can be difficult for a lot of beginners - who are often taught to catch trending Momentum-style moves. Looking for areas where the market recently bounced, and in this example, is one way to find support and resistance entries in a ranging market.

You can achieve a positive EV by entering at these levels even if your win rate is 50% and your risk-reward is even 1.1 gained per dollar risked.

Anything above that on either win rate or risk-reward ratio would give you an even better EV. One way to achieve that is to stack other factors in your favor.

MULTI-TIMEFRAME ANALYSIS

One of the best ways to increase the probability of entries near support and resistance is to look at a higher timeframe to confirm that the price action there matches your intended direction.

If your primary timeframe (where you make your trading decisions) is a 5-minute chart, you can check the 1-hour chart for a broad context.

If you focus primarily on the 4-hour chart for entries, you can check the daily chart for a broad context.

The goal is to confirm that your trade direction makes as much sense in the higher timeframe's context as it does in your primary timeframe.

PRICE ACTION REVERSAL ENTRIES

In an uptrend (higher highs + higher lows), as long as new highs are made and the retracements don't break the prior low, the uptrend is still alive.

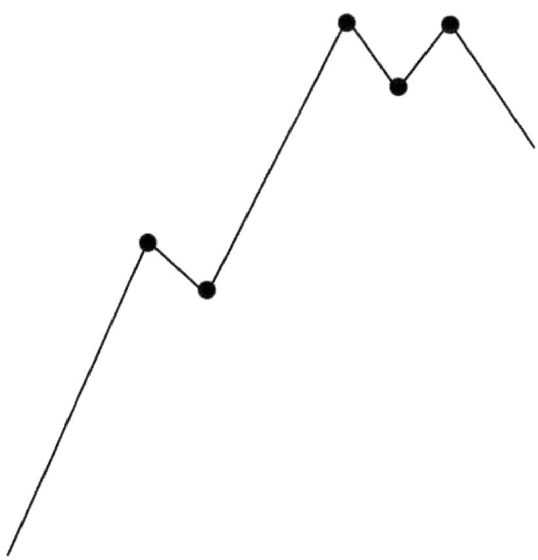

If, however, the market fails the break a new high, be alert for the break of the last bounce off a low. This is where you can find potential reversals. If the market breaks the last swing low, be on the lookout for opportunities to short sell.

On the flip side, if the current trend is a downtrend (lower lows + lower highs), then as long as new lows are made and the retracements upward do not break the prior high, you are still in a downtrend.

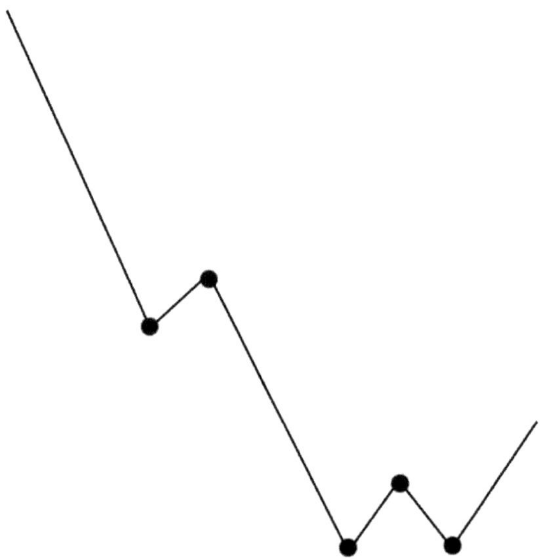

In this case, if the market fails to break down to a new low, be on the lookout for a break of the most recent high.

Once the market passes that high, look for long (buy) entries.

Remember, every market movement in relation to a previous bounce off a high, or a previous bounce off a low, acts as a test to see if those highs/lows can be broken. It's like an Amazon seller trying to test to see if they can get away with selling the product for more than before and still have buyers take the other side of the transaction.

The following is a real-life example of the first scenario, an uptrend failing to break a new high.

Many traders read this as a "double top" pattern. But if you're learning price action, it's actually clearer to recognize why that is important. Double tops actually indicate the failure of the market to find any interest in any price above the previous high.

Financial markets are a continuous dual auction process, and the auction has stalled on the way up. So, the opposite side of the dual auction process takes over and the natural next step is to test the lows to see if there will be interest below the previous low.

The following is what happened shortly after the previous image.

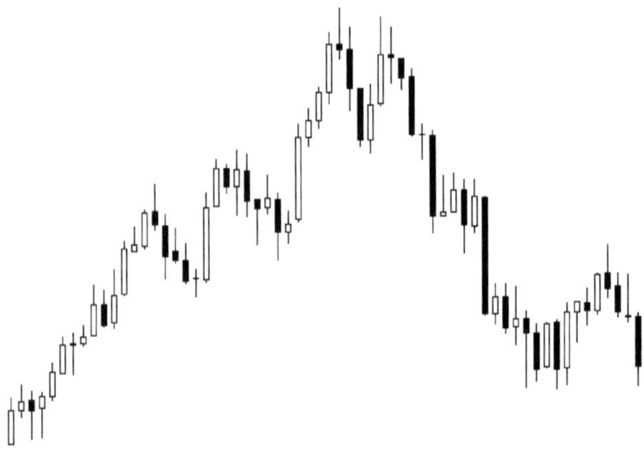

This was a 5-minute chart of the GBP/JPY (British Pounds priced in Japanese Yen.) Notice that after the "double top" (failure to break to a new high), there is a small candle that looks like a little star before the first long downward candle that confirms the reversal of the trend. That small candle signifies a lot of back and forth between market participants... until there was enough selling interest 5 minutes later, which broke that last low bounce.

When a higher low is broken, the uptrend is over.

This does not mean that the trend is also over on the 1-hour, daily, or weekly timeframes. It only means the uptrend within the 5-minute chart timeframe, which was in effect before the failure to break a new high ("double top"), has now ended.

If you are trading the 5-minute timeframe, these would be the moves you look for within the 5-minute chart. But you should check your higher timeframes to see the current context of these moves.

In reality, many "double tops" and "double bottoms" are not that clean. Sometimes, they will break a little past the first one and then reverse. Usually this results in either a "pin bar" (hammer/inverted hammer) or an engulfing pattern. Either way, these are still sometimes the beginning of a reversal but be careful with these. If you know your discipline in adhering to stop losses is good, you can attempt some of these trades too.

THE TAILWINDS TECHNIQUE

Traders often struggle to identify a clear trend in reality because real price action may look less "clear" than the examples in books.

To mitigate this, I'm presenting a way of reading price action that has helped many of the traders I've worked with over the years.

Pay attention to the tailwind side of a trend.

What do I mean by that? When an airplane is in flight, tailwinds are winds blowing from behind the plane, helping to carry the vehicle in the same direction it's already headed.

In price action, when a market is making higher highs and higher lows, the momentum is already up. So, higher highs are already happening. The Tailwinds Technique looks at the lows because every time the market moves downward and fails to break lower. The opposite is true for a downtrend.

To illustrate this concept, we'll use the Tailwinds Technique to follow a snippet of price action, with an emphasis on the tops of the candles in a downtrend.

Tailwinds Technique Illustration A

In the above image, "Tailwinds Technique Illustration A," the bottoms of the candlesticks are purposes faded so that more emphasis is placed on the top of each candle.

This is a downtrend, which is defined as lower lows and lower highs. With the Tailwinds Technique, we are paying more attention to the **lower highs**. These progressively lower highs are selling pressure pushing the downtrend along from behind - the tailwinds.

Note that the Tailwinds Technique is about **putting an emphasis on** the "push from behind" a trending move, but we don't ignore the opposite side altogether. (This is why I'm not erasing the opposite sides altogether, only fading them to provide emphasis.)

In this example, you'll notice that every candle makes a lower high until the second to last (the second candle counting from the right.) This is the first time within this example in which a high breaks higher than the previous candle's high. As the next candle (the last) shows, this break does not always mean the trend has ended.

Even though we are more focused on the tailwinds behind the trend, it's worth noting that there has **not yet been a failure** to break a new low. In the Tailwinds Technique, however, our focus is mainly on tracking the lower highs, and one previous high has been broken so far but it's not yet a full reversal.

Next, we will continue with this example and step through the price action that occurs afterward.

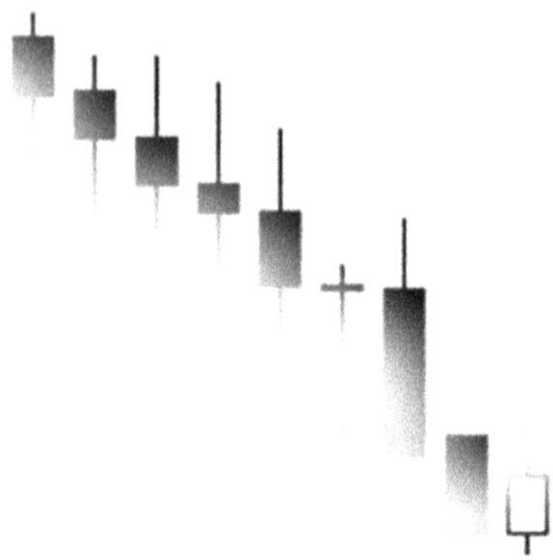

Tailwinds Technique Illustration B

Continuing from the previous illustration, we can see that the next candle does, in fact, break the high of the last candle from the previous illustration.

Without paying as much attention to the lows of the downtrend, we can still see that the first break of a high was a sign that the downtrend was weakening. This second break serves as a first confirmation. It **fails to break a lower lower** and also breaks the previous high.

Now, we are emphasizing the bottom of each candle after a potential uptrend has been signaled.

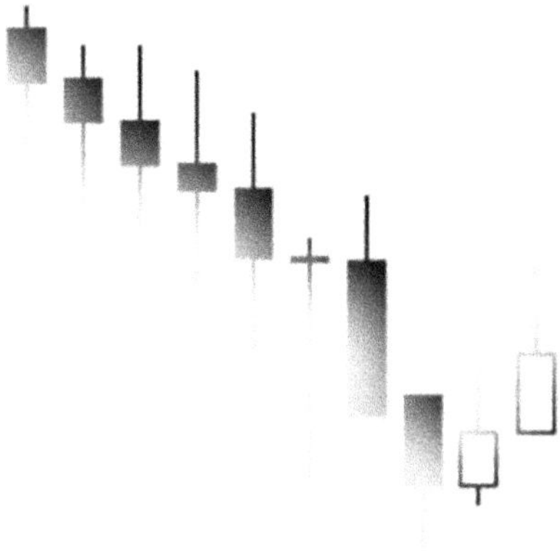

Tailwinds Technique Illustration C

Next, we begin paying more attention to the bottoms of each candle because the market looks to be breaking into an uptrend.

As long as the previous low is not broken, the new trend remains intact.

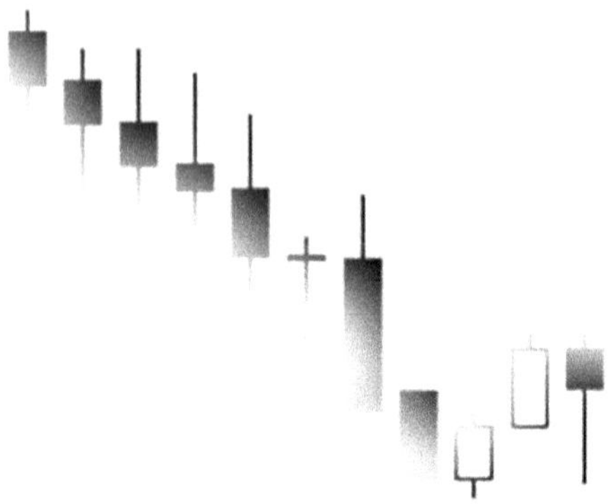

Tailwinds Technique Illustration D

The next candle does, in fact, break the previous low and also fails to break into a new high.

However, this candle (the last one in Tailwinds Technique Illustration D) breaks the previous candle's low but not the prior swing low. At this point, the failure to break to a new low from the last swing adds to the previous evidence (the breaks of highs) of the downtrend coming to an end.

This is an example of why the job of a trader isn't to predict but to react. If you see the price action up to this point, there is no real reason to feel that either direction has a greater than 50% chance of a trend-following trade. If anything, this may be the beginning of a range of consensus, but there have also not been enough bounces off the top and bottom of the range to confirm that either.

Our evidence against a confirmed trend, however,

is that the last group of candles alternate and **overlap each other** significantly. The more candles with highs and lows that overlap, the more consensus there is. **Consensus is the opposite of trending**.

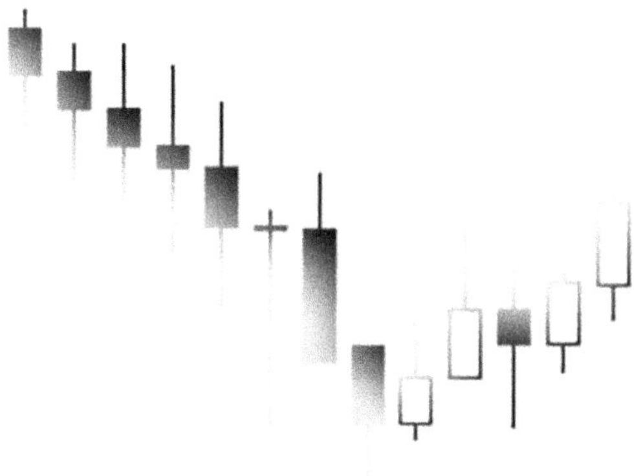

Tailwinds Technique Illustration E

With more candles continuing upward, we have one candle that breaks outside of the short-term consensus range of overlapping candles.

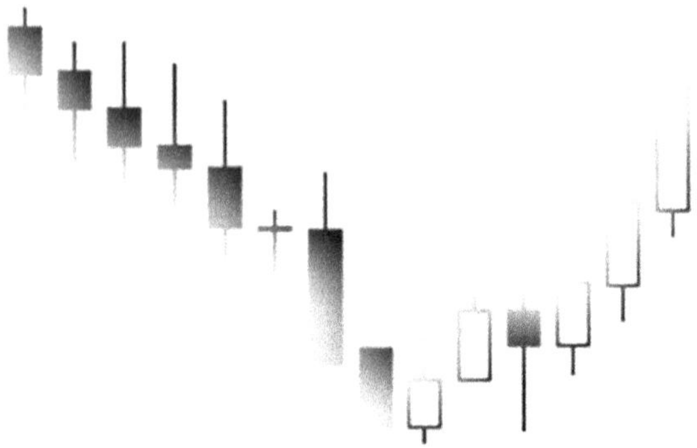

Tailwinds Technique Illustration F

In this example, the trend does reverse and continues upward. In this scenario, we can track the lows as the tailwinds behind a near-term uptrend. As long as each new low fails to break the previous low, it's an uptrend according to the Tailwinds Technique.

The Tailwinds Technique is a way to maintain a clean criterion for the continuation of trends in a particular timeframe. Use it on higher timeframes to back your decisions on lower timeframes.

It's not a predictor, and it's not a guarantee of any future price action. It's simply a way to focus on when it's time to consider that a trend is more likely to continue and when it may be weakening.

You can use the Tailwinds Technique with any type of strategy, whether you're following the trend with a momentum strategy or fading one with a mean reversion strategy.

EXAMPLE STRATEGY #1 - MOMENTUM

Here is one of the best ways to do this for a day trader:

1) Trade only during the first two hours of your instrument's main market's session. (If you trade the ES, NQ, YM, or other US futures, the New York session from 9:30am to 11:30am would be best. If you trade a GBP/USD spot or futures contract, or the FTSE index, the first two hours after 08:00 in GMT or British Summer Time would be best. If you trade the USD/JPY or Nikkei Index, the first two hours after 08:00 Japan Standard Time would be your best bet.)

This is because your prop firm challenge likely has a smaller loss limit than its profit target. You should be aiming to capture the largest possible trending move of the day in your market, and this is where you will find them.

2) Look for the first failure to break in the direction of the trend (eg. "double top" reversal of an uptrend for a short sell or "double bottom" reversal of a downtrend for a long position.)

3) Train yourself to be quick to exit for a small loss but slow to exit for a large profit.

Number 3 is the hardest part of trading. It directly goes against every natural instinct for most people. If you are trading your own capital, or if you are a hedge fund manager, you can sometimes get away with breaking this rule. In fact, it's entirely possible to be profitable taking a few larger losses as long as your win rate is high enough (it rarely is for most people but there are situations where this can be done.)

For prop firms, however, the purpose is to ensure that only disciplined traders are allowed to pass the evaluation. This is a risk management issue for the firm itself, because if you only passed the challenge due to luck, and your trading style risks large amounts per trade, the probability of you losing a lot of the firm's capital, after the pass, is much higher. So, more than in any other situation, a prop firm trader should be able to take the necessary losses.

However, be sure to understand that I'm not advocating you take losses so small that you end up killing your own chances with an extremely low win rate. There is a balance you have to find with your entries.

Being disciplined enough to take small losses doesn't mean being stupid enough to put a stop loss so close that it will get hit 90% of the time. That will cause you to lose simply because you're not giving your trades enough room to breathe (and not giving the market makers room to try to take out your stop before it continues in your favor.)

For example, if you are trading a "double bottom" reversal, you should definitely have your stop loss comfortably past the bottom of it (the low that failed to break) because the premise of your trade is only proven wrong if the market drops down and breaks that low.

Likewise, if you are short selling after a "double top" reversal, your stop loss should be comfortably above the peak of the "double top" because the premise of your trade is still valid until the market moves up again and breaks that high.

These are also highly targeted areas so the safest way to do this is to have a percent of ATR past the peak, rather than simply using the peak as your stop.

This means that for any given account size, you should be trading a number of contracts (in futures) or lot size (in forex) small enough that you can set a stop at that distance and still be within your risk limits as explained in the Risk Management chapter earlier.

The biggest challenge is that you will have to be able to let the biggest trending moves run into larger profits.

Yes, this is far more difficult to execute than it is to describe. This is because, in theory, it's how every beginner is taught. In reality, it will cause you to end up with a lot of trades where the market moves a little in your favor... then back to breakeven... then your stop loss. Or it will move a little in your favor, back to breakeven where you decide to exit, then back into profit without you on-board. Either way, these common experiences will cause you to psychologically become quick to exit winning trades.

And that is precisely the last thing you should do if you hope to succeed with a momentum strategy. (Even if you personally hate trading momentum strategies, it's worth learning to trade at least one in order to deal with strong trending market conditions.)

One compromise you can give yourself is to allow yourself to scale out of your trades. Even with a $25,000 prop firm evaluation account, you should have at least a $1500 maximum loss limit and a similar profit target (some firms even offer a symmetrical loss limit and profit target at this size), so you can still trade more than 1 Micro futures contract. Using Micro contracts, you can take half of your position at 1:1 risk-reward, and then let the remainder run.

This is not mathematically ideal for long-term profitability, but it's a compromise for traders who struggle with holding onto winning trades. As long as, on average, you take your first half at 1:1 with your risk, you should be able to maintain a positive EV.

Notice the "average" in that sentence. There are times when, with enough experience in the market, you will certainly notice the "motion" of a live market where it looks to be exhausted. It's not 100% accurate, because the participants who cause this "motion" don't know the future either, but you can develop a sense of this when you've spent enough screen time in the markets. Under such a circumstance, it may sometimes be necessary to take the partial profit a little earlier than you normally should.

The key to making this work is to be disciplined enough to really let your winners run longer when the market is offering it to you.

If you're a beginner, you should absolutely never

think this way. You're not likely to have accumulated enough experience to recognize the highest probability exhaustion moves, and you're far more likely to use this as an excuse to lock in unrealized profits.

Remember, holding onto unrealized profits - knowing that it might slip away - is a type of discomfort that you must train yourself to be okay with. It doesn't come naturally for anyone, so it takes a lot of conscious effort to train yourself to do it. It can be even harder to do than training yourself to accept losses, but it will be worth it when you succeed in doing it.

EXAMPLE STRATEGY #2 - REVERSION

1) Trade outside of the peak hours (the ones recommended in the momentum strategy)

2) Look for support/resistance areas where a reversal pattern forms. This can be the same "double top" / "double bottom" pattern or a similar reversal pattern. You might already be familiar with one that you like. The entry is not the point. There are many ways to enter, it's the context here that matters: time and being close to opposing support/resistance from a recent move.

3) Trade toward the middle of the most recent price move. Some traders consider this a 50% Fibonacci level, but it's simply the halfway point between the last bounce off a high and bounce off a low. It's even better if a clear consensus range has been established (with more than one bounce off at least one side of it) and

you can target the middle of that range.

For this type of approach, be sure that you are not trading close to a scheduled news release such as the Non-farm Payrolls or similar. You don't want to trade against new information that can massively change sentiment.

By trading inside of a range, you are trading under the premise that the current consensus in the market is approximately correct. When new information is introduced into the market, that is no longer going to be the case.

In general, this type of trade is likely to hit profit targets at a higher rate than momentum trades would, especially during ranging/consolidating market conditions, which happen more often than beginners would be led to believe.

If you have access to Volume Profile or TPO, both can be used to increase the probability of your targets. Otherwise, you can achieve a similar effect from learning to read the areas where the market has spent the most time.

If you already have a strategy that you prefer to trade and fits your view of the markets, consider some of the tips in this chapter to improve the probabilities of your strategy. Increasing the probability of any strategy is not about adding complexity. It's about taking an idea (often a relatively simple one) that applies to many situations and applying it to specific market conditions that work best with the premise of the strategy.

This is why trend-following strategies should be reserved for the most volatile times of day while mean reversion should usually be traded outside of those times.

If you keep an open mind to the information here - which is derived from over two decades of experience working with (and against) traders of all levels - you should be able to draw something from it that will improve your own strategy's success rate.

CHAPTER 10
JOURNAL YOUR TRADES

Journaling your trades is likely one of the last things you will implement. I know. It sounds unnecessary and feels like extra work. The truth is that, having worked with traders of different levels over the years, I know that many of the best traders found the most progress in their performance when they began keeping a trading journal in earnest. It works. It's that simple.

The first question you might have, of course, is why? After all, the act of trading and experiencing a win or a loss must be enough to learn everything that can be learned, right?

It may feel like it. But if you've never kept a trading journal, you may seriously be surprised at how effective it is at identifying the areas where you need improvement.

The first requirement is that you're willing to be honest with yourself.

Data to include:
- Date
- Time
- Instrument
- Quantity
- Side (Long/Short)
- P&L
- Premise (Why you chose this trade, what you expected to happen)
- Emotion (Were you anxious, angry, hesitant, etc.)
- Valid (check box)
- FOMO (check box)
- Post-Trade Notes

For every trade, log down the premise behind why you took the trade while it's still fresh in your mind. It doesn't matter if you were right or wrong, keep track of the premise of your trades.

In addition to the date, time, instrument, quantity, side (long/short), and P&L, include columns of check boxes for "valid" and "FOMO" along with any other factors you would like to track (especially if you are aware of any destructive tendencies of your own.)

If you went long because the market broke out to a new high in the session, and it's not yet close to the high of the previous day, and the daily chart is showing higher lows and higher highs, then write all of this down as the premise of the trade. If it ended up as a losing trade, it doesn't mean your premise was invalid. It's just an inevitable loss for a solid premise. Give yourself a check mark for "valid" on this trade whether it won or lost.

If, however, you took a position because you had lost before, and that was all the justification you had for the trade, then write that down... and leave the "valid" column unchecked.

Even if this invalid trade won, it was still **not** a valid trade. This type of trading is like trying to score from the opposite corner of the court after being dunked on. There's no statistical basis for expecting the trade to work out besides your own emotions.

If you are aware of your tendency to chase trending moves late, be sure to use the "FOMO" check box to track all the times you make bad entries due to fear of missing out on a big trending move. Sometimes, these will also be winners, but they're also reinforcing a habit that will lead to unnecessary losses from buying too high or shorting too low.

It's the type of behavior that's the most likely to cause you to lose even worse than you otherwise would when consolidating/ranging market conditions come around (and they inevitably will during your trading career.)

For emotion, record how you felt before the trade. Did you feel angry at the market/world? Were you nervous about taking this entry? Did you feel unsure but felt you had to take it because you might miss the move? All of this is important to log under emotion.

If your trade is based on a specific chart setup, you can include a screenshot of the chart that you used in your pre-trade analysis. This step may be more helpful to some traders than others. It depends on whether you feel highly dependent on the visuals when you trade. If you're able to describe the idea succinctly enough, you can do this entirely in the written premise of your trade.

For Post-Trade Notes, be sure to include your post-trade analysis and any other notes you may have for yourself. For example, if you took a long trade that ran directly into a major resistance level because you forgot to check a higher timeframe, then note that down in Post-Trade Notes. If you entered based on a premise that assumed it would be a big trending move, but it turned out to be a ranging day, note that down.

Many traders have a tendency to assume most days are trending days even when there has been uncertainty in the market for weeks. If you can pick up on this pattern, you might prevent yourself from assuming it will be a trending day until the market proves that premise correct first.

After you've logged your data in your trading journal, schedule periodic reviews. Look over the patterns of losing trades and invalid trades. Notice the commonalities between those trades and the emotions you logged down, the premise, the post-trade notes, etc.

You are running a business as a trader. The records of these trades are your personal records of past business activities. If you fill your journal with entries but never look at them again, you'll be missing the benefit of learning from your own mistakes.

If a convenience store decides to put a particular item at an end cap near the registers every Christmas season, and it fails to sell four years in a row, it would be a good idea not to repeat that same idea the next year. But if the owner never kept track of this data, it's more likely for the same mistake to be repeated.

By reviewing your trade journal every weekend, when both the futures and forex markets are closed for the week, you can track your progress in avoiding repeating the same types of invalid trades, chasing FOMO entries, or revenge trades.

Filtering out those errors will allow you to increase your probability of successful trades.

If you've been putting off starting your trade journal, take charge now and begin the process. Create your layout with any tool that you're familiar with, or use a ruler, pen, and paper.

It doesn't have to be perfect. It just has to do its job as the center of your accountability to your boss as a trader: yourself.

This applies equally to the prop firm evaluation stage. You may choose to do a few things differently during this phase for practical reasons, but you should still log down all of the data in your journal so you can review it after you pass or fail the evaluation challenge.

At the very least, you will have a record of the mistakes you made if you fail the evaluation. If you pass, you will have a good reference for how you may be able to improve your performance when you begin trading for real profits under the prop firm.

Remember, the markets are a game of survival of the most adaptable. Journaling your trades is an effective way to enforce your own progress and adapt to market conditions, trading strategies, and your performance with that combination. It's a form of data collection to help your future self continue to adapt and succeed.

WHERE TO GO FROM HERE

Trading is a journey of continuous learning and adaptation. Prop firm evaluation challenges are an often misunderstood opportunity for traders to access more capital and apply the skills needed to succeed. By finishing this book, you've taken the most important step toward passing your prop firm evaluation. Now, it's up to you to apply the concepts and gain real-world experience in the markets.

I founded AM Research Group to shine a light on positive EV opportunities in the markets. I invite you to become part of our growing community of better-informed traders.

Visit our website at **AMResearchGroup.com** and join our free mailing list (unsubscribe at any time) for updates, revisions to the material in this book, more trading strategy ideas for prop trading, and up-to-date insights to help you stay on the winning side of the financial markets.

ABOUT THE AUTHOR

J.T. Wellesley worked as a dealer on the trading desk of a retail forex broker then became a fund manager for a proprietary trading firm before the age of trader funding evaluation prop firms. Today, Wellesley contributes editorials with an alternative perspective on the global financial markets, manages a private capital portfolio in currencies and equity options, and founded AM Research Group (amresearchgroup.com) to continue the mission of discovering new opportunities with an edge in the markets.

www.ingramcontent.com/pod-product-compliance
Ingram Content Group UK Ltd.
Pitfield, Milton Keynes, MK11 3LW, UK
UKHW020117290926
15471UKWH00003B/192

9 798985 742923